CONTENTS – Pictorial tour of the capital city BERLIN

Brandenburg Gate 13
The new Reichstag with the visitor's dome 14, 15, 16
Federal ministerys 17
Berlins historic city centre 18, 19, 20
Friedrichstreet 21, 22, 23, 24
Potsdamer Platz and the Leipziger Street 25, 26, 27, 28, 29, 30/31
Unter den Linden – Berlin's historic boulevard 32
Bellevue Palace 33
Berlin Cathedral 34, 35, 36
Alexanderplatz, Town Hall and the Nicolai Quarter 37, 38, 39
The German Museum of Technology 40
Oberbaum Bridge /Spree, Metro No.1, Station Wahrschauer Street, Trias Buildings 41
Berlin Wall with the Checkpoint Charlie, "East-Side Gallery" .. 42, 43
Berlin-Arena, Berlin Synagoge 44, 45
The Museum Island, Pergamon-Museum 46, 47
Friedrichstadt Palace 48, 49
Statue of Victory 50
The large Festivals in Berlin 51
Berlin Zoo at Berlin-Charlottenburg 52, 53
Restaurant tour of Berlin 54/55
Emperor William Memorial Church at the Kurfürstendamm .. 56, 57
Kurfürstendamm-Boulevard 58, 59
Charlottenburg Palace 60, 61, 62
Egyptian museum/Nefertiti 63
Musical Theater of the West and the Delphi-Palace 64
Ludwig-Erhard-Building 65
ICC – International Congress Centre and Radio Tower 66, 67, 68
The Forest Theatre by the Olympic Stadium 69
Boat Trip on the Spree 70
Wannsee 71
Havel Lakes with Peacock Island 72

BERLIN
柏林・ベルリン

Publisher: HORST ZIETHEN
Introduction: JACK LANG

 ZIETHEN-PANORAMA VERLAG

© Copyright by:

ZIETHEN-PANORAMA VERLAG
D-53902 Bad Münstereifel · Flurweg 15
Telefon: 02253 - 6047 · Fax: 02253 - 6756
www.ziethen-panoramaverlag.de

Aktualisierte Auflage 2005

Redaktion und Buchgestaltung: HORST ZIETHEN

Einleitungstext: JACK LANG
(Genehmigter Nachdruck - erschienen im GEO Special Berlin)
Bildbegleitende Texte: Ziethen Panorama Verlag

Fremdsprachenübersetzungen:
ENGLISH / John Stevens · FRANÇAIS / Leïla Schenkelberg
ITALIANO / Kerstin Finco · ESPAÑOL / Dr. José García
JAPANISCH + CHINESISCH / FRANK Sprachen & Technik, Berlin

Lithografie: ZIETHEN-MEDIEN GmbH
www.ziethen.de

Gesamtherstellung:
ZIETHEN-PANORAMA VERLAG GmbH

Printed in Germany

Bildnachweis: letzte Seite

I. Dreisprachige Ausgabe: D/E/F   – ISBN 3-929932-90-3
II. Dreisprachige Ausgabe: D/Ital/Span.   – ISBN 3-929932-91-1
III. Dreisprachige Ausgabe: Chin/E/Jap.   – ISBN 3-934328-92-X

Jack Lang

柏林。人们听到这一名字,脑海里肯定会浮现出一幅幅画面:大选帝侯、胡格诺派教徒、弗里德里希(旧译为腓特烈)、伏尔泰、门德尔松、洪堡、一八四八年的街垒、格罗斯、玛琳、卡巴莱、空中桥梁中的"葡萄干轰炸机"、约翰·肯尼迪"我是柏林人"的名言、耻辱墙、东德出产的查班特小轿车……柏林不断给精神以新的食粮。柏林远不仅仅只是一个首都,柏林是我们现代史上最显著的标志之一。谁能忘却一九八九年十一月那个欧洲重新找回自己的、令人难以置信的日子?很久以前,我就已经爱上了柏林这个奇特的、迷人的城市。我之所以爱上柏林,柏林的剧院起到了主要作用。作为渴求精神食粮的年轻大学生,我来到这里朝圣,以体验布莱希特戏剧的演出。被分为两个部分的柏林为城市留下了难以承受的伤痕,但同时也为我们提供了机会,对现代戏剧中的两大纪念碑、两种模式进行对照和比较:东部的布莱希特以及舞台上的彼得·施泰因。我不断地重新回到柏林,每次来到这里内心总是充满着年轻人的热情的炙热的好奇心。每次回到这里,无论是作为电影节的主席、作为街庆的参加者或是作为偶尔来访的游客,我总会被这座城市多层次的魅力所折服。

柏林,你这闪闪发光的城市……

我爱柏林这一矛盾的城市,这一特殊的城市,不同于其它城市注重维护和谐,柏林精心维护的是其鲜明的反差。柏林从来都不是一个阿谀奉承、刻意修饰的章节,它是一个不断变化的、发展中的大都市。柏林始终渴求新兴事物,所以它始终在创造新意。柏林的景色如弗朗茨·黑瑟尔茨当年所描述的,更确切地说是"是一个小城构成的群岛",弗朗茨·黑瑟尔茨把柏林比作是一件熠熠生辉的浮雕宝石饰品。我爱这一白色城市的立体美,我爱舍内贝格区的威廉式墙面,我爱妩媚的圣湖,我爱威丁的后院式建筑,我爱绿树成荫的古纳森特林荫大道,我爱凯特-科勒惠支广场的鹅卵石路面,我爱庞大的薛尔大楼,我爱柏林中心斑斑点点的房屋,我爱国王林荫大道上富丽堂皇的别墅,我爱令赫尔姆特·纽顿迷恋的天上点点灯火,我爱万湖湖滨浴场的砂石,令

BERLIN. The name conjures up vivid images of the Great Elector Frederick William, the Huguenots, Frederick and Voltaire, Mendelssohn, the Humboldts, the barricades of the Revolution of 1848, Grosz, Marlene Dietrich, cabaret, the airlift, JFK's "Ich bin ein Berliner" speech, the Wall, the Trabant. Berlin has always given us new food for thought and food for our soul. And Berlin is more than just a capital; it is one of the most striking symbols of modern German history. Unforgettable those incredible days in 1989 when Europe was redefined. I fell in love with Berlin a long time ago, this remarkable, fascinating city. The theatre acted as intermediary. Hungry for spiritual food I made a pilgrimage here to see performances of plays by Bertolt Brecht. The partition of the city, intolerable though this division was, gave us the opportunity to compare two monuments, two models of contemporary theatre. Brecht in the east and Peter Stein at the Schaubühne. I return to Berlin regularly and am animated again and again by the same youthful enthusiasm and the same glowing curiosity. Every time I am enchanted by the magical diversity of the city, be it as President of the Film Festival, participant in the Love Parade or occasional visitor.

Berlin, the Iridescent...

I love Berlin and its contradictions, a city that cultivates contrasts as other cities cultivate harmony. It will never be a polished, spick-and-span capital, but an ever-evolving metropolis, in constant flux, constantly reinventing itself in its unquenchable thirst for innovation. With its landscape more like an archipelago of small towns as at the time of Franz Hessel, it is a lustrous cameo. I love the plastic beauty of this white city, the Wilheminian facades of Schöneberg, the grace of Heiligensee, the inner courtyards of Wedding, the shady avenues in Grunewald, the cobblestones on Käthe Kollwitz Square, the voluminous Shell building, the pock-marked houses in Berlin-Mitte, the

ベルリン。その名を聞くと目の前に鮮明なイメージが浮んでくる。大選帝侯、ユグノー派の人々、フリードリッヒ大王とヴォルテール、メンデルスゾーン、フンボルト兄弟、1848年のバリケード、グロス、マレーネ・ディートリッヒ、カバレット、「ロジーネンボンベ」と呼ばれたベルリン封鎖の際の食料空輸、「私はベルリンっ子だ」と演説したケネディー大統領、壁、トラバント車···。ベルリンは常に精神に新しい糧を与え続けてきた。ベルリンは単に首都であるだけではない。ここはわれわれの最も新しい歴史を克明にするシンボルなのだ。1989年11月のあの日、ヨーロッパが自分自身を取り戻したあの日をだれが忘れ得ようか。私は遥か昔からベルリンに、この眼を見張らせるような魅惑的な都市に惚れ込んでいた。あの頃は演劇が仲介者のような役割を演じていた。若い学生だった私は、精神的な糧に飢えて、ブレヒトの作品を上演する劇場を巡礼者のように渡り歩いていた。ベルリンが真っ二つに裂かれたことは、我々にとって耐えられないほどの衝撃だったが、そのことはかえって二つの記念塔、二つの違った現代的な演劇のモデルをお互いに比較する機会を与えてくれた。東のブレヒトと西のシャウビューネ劇団のペーター・シュタインである。私は今でもベルリンに帰って来ると、若き日の、あの同じ感激と燃えるような好奇心に取り憑かれる。あるときは映画祭の会長として、あるときはラブ・パレードの参加者として、またあるときはただの旅行者としてベルリンを訪れるとき、いつでも私はこの都市が幾重にもなげかけてくる魔法の力に屈してしまう。

玉虫色に変化するベルリンよ···

私はこの様々な矛盾を含んだベルリンを愛している。他の都市が調和を育てるのに対して、この特別な都市はコントラストを生み出す。ここは決して舐めるようにきれいに清掃された首都にはならないだろう。むしろ未来の世界都市になるべく、常に変化を遂げ続け、新しいものを渇望しつつ、その姿を更新していくことだろう。ベルリンの風景は、かつてフランツ・ヘッセルが「点在する島のような小さな町の群れ」と呼んだように、何層にも色の

我难以忘怀的还有柏林特产咖喱香肠(带炸薯条)以及柏林白啤酒(加少量红酒或者绿酒)……尽管柏林规模巨大，但出于审美和知识分子的原因，它仍然不失为一座深受闲逛者喜爱的城市。人们可这里徒步找寻瓦尔特·本杰明、库尔特·图霍尔斯基或是格特弗里德·本的足迹，这是一种无与伦比的经历、是一种激励和充实。柏林是一座幽灵的城市，这些幽灵们会在旅途上陪伴着游客：在万湖岸边我们会遇到克莱斯特，在色情游乐演出场所我们会遇到克里斯多夫·伊舍伍德，在亚历山大广场我们会遇到德布林，在暧昧的区域我们会碰到约翰·勒·卡雷，还会看到沙米索在寻找他的影子，在弗里德里希城精心护理的民宅中我们会遇见冯塔纳。

柏林是无可比拟的，任何人对柏林都没法无动于衷：或是表现出全面的惊羡和赞美或是给予毫不留情地批驳。柏林是一个激情的城市，一个极端的城市，一个放纵的城市，一个大胆的城市，一个在欢乐时光和在沮丧时光都勇于挑战的城市。柏林具有精神、心灵和性格。柏林是可变的、不可捉摸的、神秘莫测和缄默的。柏林是一个奇怪的城市，它喜欢维护破碎的、逆反的东西，它喜欢维护自己的对立面。柏林二十二层楼高的德比斯大楼设计者—雷措·皮亚诺曾宣称"一座城市的美丽源自于它的矛盾"，如果他的这一说法准确的话，那么柏林就达到了美学中的至高境界。匈牙利小说家彼得·伊斯特哈吉认为："这座城市的魅力就在于它的丑陋"，我却认为柏林的吸引力是以时代和风格上的富有创意的冲突为基础的。

人们只要到粮仓区或莫阿比特区的街道上去走走就会切身感受到柏林的反差，漫步时目光所及总会带给您新的意外。这里到处都是纷繁多姿的迷人景致，虽然这些景致有时让人难以理解。尽管诸如弗里德里希大街、菩提树下大街以及帝王大道等直线型交通要道妨碍了柏林城市规划的宏伟性，但最能代表和体现柏林城市风貌的确是不连贯的曲线线条。

sumptuous villas on the Königsallee, the radiant sky so fascinating to Helmut Newton, the sand at the Wannsee lido, not forgetting Currywurst (with chips) and Berliner Weisse (beer with syrup). Despite its size, Berlin is a city for strolling – for aesthetic and intellectual reasons. Here you can trace the footsteps of Walter Benjamin, Kurt Tucholsky or Gottfried Benn, a uniquely stimulating and enriching experience. Berlin is a city of ghosts accompanying the visitor's every step. We meet Kleist on the shores of the Wannsee, Christopher Isherwood in wicked music halls, Döblin on Alexanderplatz, John Le Carré in twilight zones, Chamisso looking for his shadow and Fontane in the elegant patrician dwellings of Friedrichstadt.

Berlin the incomparable leaves nobody indifferent. It demands undivided admiration or pitiless rejection. It is a city of passions, of extremes, of excesses, of daring, provocative in all senses of the word. It is the city of intellect, of the heart and has character. It is changeable, unpredictable, mysterious and secretive. Berlin is a paradox, a city of ruptures and U-turns that makes a point of cultivating its contrasts. If it is true what Renzo Piano says, master of the huge debus-building on Potsdamer Platz, that "The beauty of a city is the fruit of its contradictions", then Berlin is the very epitome of aestheticism. The Hungarian novelist Péter Esterházy claims that "The city's ugliness is the source of its charm." My feeling is that the city's attraction lies in the productive confrontation of epochs and styles. You only have to wander through the streets of the Scheunenviertel or Moabit to become aware of the contrasts that catch the eye again and again. It is this diversity that is so captivating, even if it is not always easy to understand. And although upright straight thoroughfares like Friedrichstrasse, Unter den Linden and Kaiserdamm disturb its grand design, it is the broken line that represents this city best.

変化するカメオにも喩えられる。私はこの白亜の都市の柔軟な美しさが好きだ。シェーネベルクのヴィルヘルム風のファサード、ハイリゲンゼーの優雅さ、ヴェディングの裏庭、鬱蒼としたグリューネヴァルトの通り、ケーテ・コロヴィッツ広場の玉砂利の石畳、巨大なシェル・ビル、中央区のあばたのような家並み、ケーニヒスアレーに並ぶ瀟洒な邸宅、ヘルムート・ニュートンを魅了してやまなかった大空の輝き、ヴァン湖畔の砂が好きだ。そして忘れてはならないのがフライド・ポテトを添えたカレー・ソーセージとちょっとシロップを入れたベルリーナー・ヴァイス・ビール・・・。ベルリンはとても大きな街だが、ブラブラと歩き回る人々にふさわしい町でもある。彼らは芸術と知性の故に町中を放浪するのである。この町で人々はヴァルター・ベンヤミン、クルト・トゥホルスキー、そしてゴットフリート・ベンの足跡を求めて彷徨うのだ。それはまたとない、刺激的で豊満な体験となる。ベルリンは幽霊の町だ。車に乗っているといつの間にか幽霊が横に座っている。ヴァン湖畔ではクライストに、いかがわしい寄席ヴァリエテではクリストファー・イシャーウッドに、アレクサンダー広場ではデブリーンに会える。ジョン・レ・カレは薄暗がりに潜み、シャミッソーは自分の影を探している。フォンテーヌはフリードリッヒシュタットの手入れの行き届いた民家にいる。

ベルリンは類いなき街であり、他の都市の追随を許さない。ベルリンはあなたを惹きつけてやまないか、手厳しく撥ねつけるかのどちらかだ。ここは情熱の街であり、良きにつけ悪しきにつけ極端で、過激で、野望にあふれ、挑発する街である。ここには精神と心と個性がある。この街は絶えず変化し、予測がつかず、秘密めいて寡黙だ。ベルリンはパラドックスに満ち、傷を抱え、180度転換を遂げる都市だ。だれかが気に入ったと思えばその反対を提示してくる。22階建てのデビス・ハウスを設計したレンツォ・ピアノが語った、「都市の美しさはその矛盾の中から生まれてくる」という言葉が正しければ、ベルリンは美の最先端にいることになる。ハンガリーの小説家ペーター・エステルハージーは、「この町の魅力はその醜さにある」と主張した。

柏林，你这高雅的城市……

对我来说，柏林是一个质朴中不乏优雅、高尚与无耻合为一体的、神秘莫测的女子。她的历史上曾出现过拉尔、罗莎、艾尔瑟、克莱尔、玛琳、希尔德加德、卡特琳等等。一个柏林能够掩饰一个另外的、许多另外的柏林。人们说巴黎始终就是巴黎，但柏林从来不会就是柏林。抓不到摸不着、瞬息万变以及矛盾百出，这就是柏林迷一般美丽的地方。柏林并不引诱，而是征服。她并不使人入迷，而是使人入魔。柏林让人无法归类，柏林让人无法断论，所以柏林的多样性根本无法减少。柏林有如一点鬼火，刺激着人们的思想。人们认为自己理解了它，但它又展示了一幅新的面孔，使人迷惑不解，让人不知所措。这种情况也许能够解释为什么柏林是一个游荡着从劳拉—劳拉到达米尔等众天使的天使城。柏林始终是"沸腾的锅炉"，这是本世纪初哈瑞·克斯勒的诅咒，克劳斯·曼曾这样描述柏林这座城市"在让人同情的同时又让人着迷：灰色、破烂、堕落，但生命力却在焦躁不安地跳动；闪闪发光、熠熠生辉、点点鬼火、狂热刺激、高度紧张却能给您承诺"。

柏林喜欢这种不稳定的平衡，因为这就是生活本身。柏林就象一个走钢丝演员。被恩斯特·刘别谦赋予美誉的柏林守护神具有多面性：她有巨大的生存意志、有对现代风格无法抑制的欲望、对所有新事物的强烈偏爱，一种嘲讽的、挑战性的无畏无敬以及宽容和好客的特性。十七世纪，柏林宽容和好客的特性尤其被法皇路易十四从法国驱赶出来的上千胡格诺派教徒受益匪浅。因此，对法国人来说，柏林具有如此重要的意义。尽管柏林有时显得如此异样，也就是作家沃尔夫冈·布希尔说的"古怪"，但外来人在这一城市中不会感到陌生。柏林之所以吸引人，因为它是各种人、各种知识过渡、混杂以及相会的地方。对外开放是柏林的主要任务。我感到非常高兴，除了土耳其人、希腊人、意大利人以及来自俄罗斯的犹太人重新找到了通往柏林的道路，奥拉宁堡大街周围地区又复兴到本世纪初的景象。柏林确实起到了沟通东西方的桥梁作用。柏林是一个世界性城市。柏林是一个各种设想和试

Berlin, the Elegant...

For me Berlin is a woman full of mystery, natural and elegant, magnanimous and impertinent all at the same time. It bears the features of Rahel, Rosa, Else, Claire, Marlene, Hildegard, Katharina... One Berlin can mask another, many others. Paris always remains Paris, but Berlin never stays Berlin. The mysterious beauty is so difficult to grasp, so fleeting, so paradoxical. She doesn't seduce, she conquers. She doesn't enchant, she puts a jinx on you. Berlin cannot be defined, its diversity is simply not to be reduced to a common denominator. It is a mirage, a miracle that excites our senses and teases our minds. You think you've begun to understand her, but then she reveals a new feature, misleads you and causes confusion. It is this peculiarity that perhaps explains why Berlin has always been home to angels, from Lola-Lola to Damiel. Berlin remains the seething cauldron conjured up by Harry Kessler at the beginning of the 20th century, a city "both piteous and seductive: grey, shabby, run down, yet vibrant with nervous vitality, glistening, glittering, phosphorescent, hectic and animated, full of tension and promise", as Klaus Mann once described it. Berlin feels comfortable with this unstable balance, it is its very lifeblood. Berlin is a tightrope walker. Berlin's genius, expressed so wonderfully by Ernst Lubitsch, is multi-facetted: an enormous will to live, an uncontrollable appetite for modernity, an inclination towards all that is new, a mocking, provocative lack of respect and a tolerance and hospitality from which thousands of Huguenots profitted in the 17th century having been driven out of France by Louis XIV.

That is why Berlin has a special meaning for the French. Although Berlin sometimes seems so strange, so foreign, so "bizarre", as the writer Wolfgang Büscher put it, a stranger never feels forlorn in this city. It is welcoming, having always been a place of transition, a melting pot both in human terms and intellectually.

私はベルリンの魅力はむしろそれぞれの時代と様式における対比が生み出した創造性にあると思っている。はっきりとしたコントラストを見たければ、ショイネン地区かモアビート地区に行ってみるとよい。そこで見られる新奇さにはいつも驚かされる。理性はすぐにこのような多様性を受け入れられないかもしれないが、魅了されることは確かである。フリードリッヒ通り、ウンター・デン・リンデン、カイザーダムといった真直ぐな幹線道路は、寛大な都市設計を邪魔しているが、それはまさにベルリンを最もよく表現する壊れた線なのだ。

優雅なベルリンよ···

私にとってはベルリンという都市は、飾り気のなさとエレガントさが、あるいは気高さと鼻っぱしの強さが入り混じったような魅力溢れる女性のようである。時に応じて、かつて歴史に名を残した多くの女性たち、ラヘル、ローザ、エルゼ、クレール、マレーネ、ヒルデガート、カタリーナ···などの容貌を見せ、多くの秘密を隠している。パリが常にパリであるのとは違って、ベルリンは決していつも同じベルリンではありえない。どこか掴みどころがなく、うつろいやすく、互いに反目しあうものを同時に持ち続ける、そんな謎めいた美を兼ね備えている。誘惑者ではなく、征服者であり、魔法使いではなく、魔女のようなのである。ベルリンの姿をはっきり見定めることも、決まった名前で呼ぶこともできないほどこの都市は多様性に富んでいる。ベルリンは人間の五感を奮い立たせ、悟性を刺激するような驚くべき所であり、理解したと思ったとたんに別の姿を表し、全てを煙に巻いてしまうような不思議な都市でもある。この特性は、ベルリンがロラロラからダミエルまでなぜ天使の居所なのかを説明しているだろう。ベルリンは今もハリー・ケスラーが今世紀の始めに語った「煮え立ったやかん」であり、クラウス・マンがかつて言ったように「情け深い心と誘惑する心を同時に持ち合わせ、色褪せて見すぼらしく、腐敗している一方で、神経質なまでのバイタリティーに活気づき、あるときは燦然と輝き、あるときは淡い光を放ち、せっかちに活動するようなスリルと希望に満ちあふれている町である」。この

验的大型实验室。柏林不仅属于柏林居民,而且属于所有感到与柏林具有千丝万缕联系的人,属于所有为能生活在自由之中而心存感激的人。

我们都是柏林人。柏林这一城市拥有取之不尽的能量,它能不断地重新站起来,重新复活。柏林能从所面临的严峻考验中吸取新的力量。凭借着旺盛的生命力,柏林经受住了工业化时代的破坏、战争的严重破坏以及被分割成东西柏林所留下的伤害。柏林的吸引力也正是在于其挑战一切的能力之中。挑战越大,柏林也就越果敢。柏林在过去的世纪中什么也不缺乏。

柏林,你这古怪的城市……

柏林特殊之处在于它在撤退和奋起的历史之间、在忘却和记忆之间辩证的紧张关系。这种紧张挑起了激烈的争论,就象人们在围绕着重建柏林城市宫殿所进行的讨论中见到的那样。但这不会导致瘫痪和僵化,相反,它会产生一种创造性的推动力。柏林与八十年代被画满彩色图画的柏林墙非常相似:它像是一张巨大的、波特莱尔风格的羊皮纸。此外,让我感到非常遗憾的是,出于非常容易理解的愿望,这一给人带来痛苦回忆的伤疤被从城市画面上迅速抹去了,柏林墙的大部分没能得以保存,不然可让后代更好地了解冷战的疯狂和迷乱。因为作为纪念碑再没有比在事件原发地的实物更成功、更具震撼力和影响力了。

Its main task is to open itself to outside influences. I am pleased that Jews of Russian origin have found their way to Berlin again, to join the Turks, the Greeks and the Italians, and to bring back to life the area round Oranienburger Strasse as they did at the turn of the century. Berlin has indeed the function of a bridge between east and west. Berlin is a metropolis. It serves as a laboratory for ideas and experiments. It belongs not only to those who live here, but to all who feel attached to it, all those who owe their life in freedom to the city. We are all Berliners. This city has limitless resources of energy, enabling it to resurrect itself time and again. It gains new strength from the trials and tribulations it has overcome. Thanks to its creative vitality, it overcame the destruction of the industrial age, the devastations of war and the injuries of partition. Therein lies its attraction: in its ability to face all challenges. The larger it is, the greater its determination.

Berlin, the Bizarre...

What makes the city so special is the dialectic relationship to history, somewhere between retreat and revolt, between forgetting and remembering. This tension produces controversies, such as that, for example, the rebuilding of the city castle. But it does not lead to paralysis or ossification. On the contrary, it produces a creative, animating dynamism. Year day after end of war. Berlin is like the brightly coloured wall of the 80s: a gigantic, Baudelarian Palimsest. Actually I find it regrettable that the understandable desire to remove the painful scar from the face of the city as quickly as possible has meant that so little of the wall has been preserved, which would have made it easier for future generations to grasp the aberrations of the Cold War. No monument, however successful, commands the same suggestive power as a real place.

人生そのもののような二面性がベルリンの魅力であり、「綱渡り曲芸師」を見ているようだ。エルンスト・ルービチュが見事に表現したように、ベルリンの魅力には多くの側面がある。人生に対する激しい意志、現代に関する堪え難いまでの好奇心、新しいもの全般に対する好み、人を嘲るような、あるいは挑発的なまでの不遜な態度、そして特に17世紀にルイ14世によってフランスから追放され、逃げてきたユグノーたちを受け入れることを許した厚意と寛大さである。このため、ベルリンはフランス人にとっては特別な意味を持つ。このように時としてベルリンは「奇妙な」印象を与えるにも関わらず、作家のヴォルフガング・ビューシャーには「ベルリンではよそ者がよそ者と感じられなくなる」と思えたという。ベルリンはずっと以前から出会いの場所であり、人々が混ざりあい、あるいは通り過ぎていく場所であったために、どんな人でも招き入れのである。常に外に向って門戸を開くことがベルリンの主要な任務であるのだ。私がとても嬉しいと思っているのは、トルコ人、ギリシア人、イタリア人の他にもロシア出身のユダヤ人が再びベルリンにやってくるようになったこと、そしてオラーニエンブルク通りの辺りが前世紀の初頭のような活気を取り戻したことである。ベルリンは実際に東西の橋渡しをしている世界都市であり、新しい思想や試みのための「実験室」のような役割も果たしている。ベルリンは決してそこに住む人たちだけのものではなく、ベルリンとつながりを持つ全ての人々のもの、自由な人生を送る人々全てのものである。

だから私たちは全員「ベルリンっ子」である。ベルリンには再び立ち上がり、復活することを可能にするような強大なエネルギーが常に備わっている。ベルリンは負わされた試練の中から新たな力を創り出す。この新しいものを創り出すバイタリティーのおかげで産業時代の非人間性や戦争による荒廃、そして東西ドイツの分断の痛みを乗り切って来た。あらゆる試練を自らに課すことができる点にベルリンの魅力がある。その試練が大きければ大きいほど、ベルリンは断固としてそれに立ち向かい、かつて一度もその試練に負けたことがなかった。

柏林，你这遍体鳞伤的城市……

冷战从柏林开始，也在柏林结束。这一历史是我们的历史，这是一部将我们团结和连接在一起的历史，这部历史有苦痛也有欢乐。这部历史对我们的现实生活产生了深刻的影响。这部历史是欧洲东西方民众共有的民主思想生长的沃土。这一历史的引发点之一是所谓的空中桥梁，这是一场不同寻常的人道主义援助活动，它将德国和西方世界紧密地连接在一起。一九九八年举行了庆祝柏林空中桥梁五十周年的纪念活动。当年，柏林结束了与军国主义以及大普鲁士主义的认同，并从此发展成为一个和平卫士的标志。当年的空中桥梁不仅输送了柏林急需的食品和煤炭，这座空中桥梁上还形成了我们的文化。
空中桥梁是全体欧洲人民的胜利。

柏林，你这令人感到恐惧的城市……

柏林与历史的关系极为紧张。柏林是在十九世纪以异乎寻常的速度发展起来的勃兰登堡城市，这座城市对我们的时代产生了如此深刻的影响，以至于我们可以说，柏林体现了二十世纪所受的所有苦难、所有内心矛盾以及最惨烈的悲剧，当然，柏林也呈现了二十世纪所带来的所有美好事物、所有梦幻和惊喜。柏林是我们历史和我们欧洲大陆的一个缩影，这一缩影既让我们感到非常震惊，又让我们十分赞叹和惊羡。我个人对柏林的齐默街情有所锺，齐默街是波茨坦广场上的一条小街。这个地方是柏林历史、德国历史乃至欧洲历史的一个聚光镜：这里在马丁-格鲁皮乌斯大楼的对面是普鲁士州议会；在过去把柏林一分为二的柏林墙的另一面是戈林的帝国航空部（过去德意志民主共和国政府部门所在地和今天的德意志联邦共和国财政部所在地），边上还有德国党卫军总部和盖世太保总部这两个令人毛骨悚然的地点。这是怎样一幅场景！柏林墙

Berlin, the Scarred...

The Cold War began in Berlin. And the end came in Berlin, too. This bit of history is our history, our shared, sometimes painful, sometimes happy history, uniting us all. It defines our present. It is the humus on which democratic ideals thrive, shared by the peoples of eastern and western Europe alike. One of the starting points of this story was the airlift, this incredible humanitarian campaign that strengthened the ties between Germans and the western world and whose 50th anniversary was celebrated in 1998. Berlin's identification with militarism and Prussian ideals ceased, it became the modern symbol of the defence of liberty. The airlift not only brought food and coal, hope came out of the sky over Berlin, hope that our civilisation now rests on. The airlift was a victory for all Europeans.

Berlin, the Frightening...

Berlin's relationship to history is one of tension. The Brandenburg city and its explosive growth in the 19th century has so shaped our epoch that one could say Berlin is the embodiment of the 20th century, with all its sufferings, its divisions and its most grievous tragedies, but also with the beauty it brought with it, all its dreams and surprises. Berlin is a mirror image of our history and of our continent, a source of dismay but also admiration. I personally have an especially soft spot for Zimmerstrasse, a little street of the Potsdamer Platz. It is the essence of Berlin's history, and thus Germany's and Europe's too. The Prussian State Parliament stands opposite the Martin Gropius building, on the other side of the wall that once divided the city, Göring's airforce ministry (former seat of GDR ministeries and future seat of the Finance Minister), the topography of terror with the headquarters of the SS and the Gestapo. What a sight! The redesign of the city since the fall of the wall is impressive. The work created on the banks of the Spree is

奇妙なベルリンよ・・・

ベルリンの特異性は、暴動と撤退、あるいは忘却と追憶の歴史に対する弁証法的関係にあるといえる。このように対立する概念から、王宮の再建をめぐる問題をどう捉えるかについての議論が醸し出されるが、そのために身動きが取れなくなってしまう、ということはない。むしろ反対にダイナミズムが生まれてくるのだ。ベルリンは80年代のあの、カラフルな壁によく似ている。それはまるで巨大なボーデュレ風のパリムプセスト（書いてあった文字を消して再使用した羊皮紙あるいはパピルスによる写本）で、ひとたび生じた波紋を全て取り込み、そしてただちに記憶から消し去ってしまうかのようだ。私がとても遺憾に思うのは、ベルリンの町から今尚痛々しい傷跡を一刻も早く消し去りたいという、至極もっともな望みのために、後に続く世代が冷戦時代の過ちを具体的に理解できるベルリンの壁を、ほんの僅かしか残さずに撤去してしまったことである。ベルリンの壁ほど雄弁な歴史の証人はいないからだ。

傷だらけのベルリンよ・・・

冷戦はベルリンで始まった。そしてその終結はやはりベルリンで迎えた。この歴史はわれわれみんなの歴史であって、だれにでも共有されるべきで、時には痛みを感じさせ、そして時には喜びをかみしめさせる歴史なのである。この歴史を通してわれわれは結びつけられ、一つとなるのだ。この歴史はわれわれの現在に刻みつけられている。この歴史が土壌となって、西ヨーロッパと東ヨーロッパに共通する民主主義を養ったのだ。この歴史の一つの出発点となったのはベルリン空輸だろう。このヒューマニズムに基づいた行動がドイツと西側諸国との結びつきを深めることになり、1998年にはベルリン空輸50周年を祝った。あの頃ベルリンは軍国主義を廃止し、プロイセンと同一視されることを避けるようになった。そして、それ以来自由の擁護者として現代のシンボルとなった。ベルリン空輸によってもたらされたのは食料や燃料だけでなく、上空から希望が舞い降りて来たのだ。それはドイツ

被推倒后，这个城市的重新塑造工作给人留下了深刻的印响。施普雷河畔完成了恢宏的作品，尽管这一方案并非人人喜欢，但它使我的内心充满了惊羡和赞美。而且这一建筑学上的变化代表了柏林的传统—引入和使用全新的手法和要素。

柏林，你这令人惊羡和赞美的城市……

柏林这一政治城市的根本变化提出了一个痛苦的问题，这一问题让德国上下以及报刊杂志都陷入深深地思索之中：对柏林和柏林共和人们有必要感到害怕吗？法国的共和是按照笛卡尔学说编号的，与法国相反，德国人把共和加在一个城市的名称上，更多的只是为了富含诗意而已：在魏玛和波恩之后，现在轮到了柏林。这些名字按照马丁·瓦尔泽的说法"只不过是一张标签"，我们应将这些名字作为一种意愿的表述方式来理解，五十年的内心矛盾，不仅柏林和德国，就是欧洲也有必要克服。因此，对我来说，德国首都从莱茵河畔（距法国只有很短一段距离）迁移到施普雷河畔（距波兰只有八十公里）就像德国重新统一、重新统一的标志以及具体实施迁都规划一样，都是自然而然、顺理成章的。此外，迁都柏林还有其现实意义，它有助于建立新的平衡，这种平衡是欧洲在过去十五年中重新找回的。柏林曾是一个分裂的欧洲大陆的象征，现在它已成为一个正在找回自己的新欧洲的标志。

柏林，你这内心自相矛盾的城市……

德国首都从波恩迁都柏林既不涉及到德国与西方世界建立稳固的关系问题，也不牵涉到它加入某一欧洲组织的关键之举。德国民主的联邦制结构既证明了它的稳定性、又证实了它的透明性。新的国会大厦将稳定和透明这两种特性有机地结合在一起。诺曼·弗斯特在保罗·瓦洛特设计改建的巨大基座上，给新的国会大厦冠以一个熠熠生辉的、透明玻璃穹顶。

gigantic and fills me with admiration, even if the idea of a "critical reconstruction" that enjoys not everyone. Architectural change has always been part of the Berlin tradition of adding new elements to a determinedly disparate whole.

Berlin, the Admired…

The political move to Berlin and the transition it signals throws up the nagging question that has been occupying minds and the newspapers on both sides of the Rhine: should one be afraid of the Berlin Republic? In contrast to the French custom of numbering their republics in a Cartesian formula, Germans give theirs the names of cities, which is much more poetic: so after Weimar and Bonn, it's Berlin's turn. This name, according to Martin Walser "just a label", must be understood as the expression of a wish. To overcome 50 years of conflict and division, not just of Berlin and of Germany, but of the whole of Europe. So moving the country's capital from the banks of the Rhine (just a stone's throw from France) to the banks of the Spree (80 kilometres from Poland) seems to me just as natural as German reunification, of which the move is both the symbol and the materialization. It also signals a realization of the new reality and the new balance that Europe has rediscovered in the last 15 years. Berlin was the symbol of a divided continent, now it is an emblem of a new Europe searching for itself.

Berlin, the Torn…

Moving the capital raises a question mark neither about Germany's firm base in the west, nor about its determined advocation of a European "house". The federally structured German democracy has proven its stability as well as its transparency, they have in common with the new Reichstag, in which Paul Wallot's massive base is crowned by Norman Foster's shining, transparent dome.

の文化の基盤となった希望だった。ベルリン空輸はヨーロッパ全体にとっての勝利だったのだ。

ハラハラさせるベルリンよ・・・

ベルリンの歴史に対する態度は物凄く緊張していた。既に19世紀から目覚ましく発達していたブランデンブルク州の都市であったベルリンは、誰も想像できないほどわれわれの時代に克明な特徴を刻み込んだ。この都市は20世紀の悲しみ、分裂、最悪の悲劇を体現するかのようであるが、同時に多くの美しさを備え、夢と驚きをいっぱいに抱いている。ベルリンはドイツの歴史とドイツ全土の縮小図であり、われわれを狼狽させたり驚嘆させたりする。私はツィンマーマン通りにひとかたならぬ思い入れがある。そこはポツダム広場の小さな通りなのだが、ベルリンの、ドイツの、またヨーロッパの歴史を凝縮したような場所なのだ。この通りにはマルティン・グロピウス館の向い側にプロイセンの国会議事堂があった。そして、かつてベルリンを二つに裂いていた壁の向こう側にゲーリンクの航空省があった（旧東独の内閣のあったところで、現在は大蔵省が置かれている）。そこはナチスの親衛隊とゲシュタポの司令部であり、恐怖の一角であった。なんという光景だろうか。ベルリンの壁が崩壊してからの都市の改造には眼を見張るものがある。シュプレー河のほとりに完成した建築物は巨大であり、私をすっかり虜にする。そのコンセプトがすべての人間の気に入らないものであったとしてもである。けれども、このような建築の転換こそがベルリンの伝統なのであり、雑然とより集められた中に新しい要素が付け加えられているのだ。

感嘆されるべきベルリンよ・・・

政治と都市の根本的な改革は、ライン河の両岸で頭を悩ませ、新聞が騒ぎ立てるような大きな問題を投げかけた。ベルリンとベルリン共和国に恐れを抱く必要があるだろうか。それぞれの共和制にデカルト式に順番に番号をつけて呼ぶフランスと違って、ドイツではそれぞれの共和国に都市の名前をつける。その方がずっと詩的に響

柏林，你这欧洲化的城市……

柏林不仅将改变德国的画面，而且还将改变其执政者的思想。与舒适的联邦小村庄波恩相比，大都市的生活将形成另一幅世界性画面。柏林的执政者将更加贴近地了解德国人、尤其是新联邦州百姓的日常担忧和困扰，同时能够更好地理解世界上的问题。他们将获得一个开放的、世界性的、现代化的"首都文化"，并使柏林成为名符其实的文化首都，成为屠格涅夫曾经赞誉的欧洲生活的精神中心。当前的最大任务是将东德年轻的民主整合到欧洲文化空间中。对此，柏林能够提供一些关键的优势：柏林具有三座大型歌剧院、几乎五十座戏剧院、远远超过一百家博物馆、二百家电影院、二百家美术馆，这还不包括柏林思如泉涌的标新立异者，如大众舞台上的弗朗克·卡斯托弗斯、德国戏剧界的托马斯·朗格霍夫或是年轻的、擅长于推陈出新的托马斯·沃斯特玛雅。

选择柏林作为德国首都，引用历史学家弗里茨·施特恩的评论，是"一个新的开端"。但这也是一种挑战和希望：要将四分五裂的边界整合成一个统一的欧洲是一项巨大的挑战，建立一个统一的、稳定的、繁荣的、和平的欧洲是一个美好的希望。柏林的吸引力将成为欧洲大陆稳定的中心。柏林需要欧洲，欧洲也需要柏林。德国首都是一个充满想象的、富有创意的、开放的、执著的欧洲神经中心。柏林是了解多层次的、富饶的欧洲文化的好地方。

Berlin, the European…

Berlin will change the image of Germany and the thinking of those in government. A different view of the world will evolve during life in the metropolis, different from Bonn, the cosy government "village". They will be closer to the daily cares of Germans especially in the former GDR, and at the same time will understand worldwide problems better. They will develop a capital culture, which is more open, more cosmopolitan, more modern, worthy of a cultural capital which Turgenev lauded as a refuge of European life. One of the great tasks of today is the integration of the young democracies of the east into European civilization. Berlin has a few important trumps up its sleeve: three large opera houses, nearly 50 theatres, well over 100 museums, 200 cinemas, 200 galleries, not to mention people of the ilk of Frank Castorf at the Volksbühne, Thomas Langhoff at the Deutsches Theater or the young Thomas Ostermeier, people brimming over with ideas.

The choice of Berlin as the new capital is "a new start", to use a phrase coined by the historian Fritz Stern. But it is also a challenge and a promise: a challenge to integrate a disparate whole, and a promise of a united, solidaric, flourishing and peaceful Europe. The attractive force of Berlin will become a pole of stability on our continent. Berlin and Europe need each other. The capital of Germany is one of the nerve centres of an inventive, creative, open, individualistic Europe. Berlin is the right place to experience the diversity and wealth of European civilization and its invaluable culture.

くと思う。ヴァイマールとボンの次にはベルリンがくるのだ。マルティン・ヴェルザーに言わせると「単なるラベル」に過ぎないのだが、われわれはこれらの都市の名前を希望の表れとして受けとめるとしよう。50年間にわたる分裂、それはベルリン、ドイツ、いや、ヨーロッパ全体の分裂なのだが、その悲劇を克服しようとしているのだ。それだから、フランスからほんの少ししか離れていないライン河畔から、ポーランドから80キロメートル離れた所にあるシュプレー河畔に首都を移転するということは、ドイツの統一を回復し、それを象徴し、かつ具体的に示すという目的のためには当然のことと思われる。それは新しい現実とヨーロッパがこの15年間に再発見した均衡を実現化していくことをも知らせている。ベルリンは引き裂かれたヨーロッパ大陸を体現するものであり、現在新しく自分自身を探究しているヨーロッパのシンボルなのである。

引き裂かれたベルリンよ・・・

首都の移転は、ドイツが西ヨーロッパへ回帰するということでも、ヨーロッパ共同体へ参加することが明白になるということでもない。連邦的な構造を持ったドイツ国家の民主性は既に証明済みだ。新しい帝国議事堂はパウル・ヴァロッツによる巨大な骨組みとノーマン・フォスターによる透明で光り輝く丸天井を持っている。その二つの特徴は、ドイツの新しい国家の性質にそっくり当てはまるようだ。

ヨーロッパ人であるベルリンよ・・・

ベルリンはドイツのイメージやドイツの政治家たちの考えを変革していくだろう。ベルリンのような大都市での生活は、今までのこじんまりとした首都ボンでの生活とは全く異なる世界像を作り上げるだろう。特に旧東独地域の国民の日々の憂いをもっと身近に感じると同時に、世界規模の諸問題をよりよく理解するようになるだろう。そして、はるかに開放的で、コスモポリタニズムにあふれ、現代的で、ヨーロッパ的生活の宝として文豪ツルゲーネフを賞賛するような文化都市に相応しい本物の「

大约一六五五年的柏林一科恩图。铜版画作者N·维斯切
Ansicht von Berlin-Cölln um 1655. Radierung von N. Vischer
1655年頃のベルリン・ケルンの眺めN.フィッシャー作のエッチング

首都文化」を身につけるだろう。東欧の若き民主主義国家をヨーロッパ文化圏に統合することは目下の主要課題の一つである。ベルリンはそのための奥の手をいくつか持っている。3つのオペラハウス、50の劇場、100を越える美術館や博物館、200の映画館、200のギャラリー、そして思想の輝きに満ちたフォルクス・ビューネ(国民劇場)のフランク・カストルフやドイツ劇場のトーマス・ラングホーフ、あるいは若きトーマス・オースターマイヤーといった偶像破壊主義者たちである。

ベルリンを新生ドイツの首都に選ぶことは、歴史学者のフリッツ・シュテルンの言葉を借りれば、「新しい始まり」である。しかしそのことは同時に異なるものを全体として統合することへの挑戦と、一丸となって繁栄し、平和なヨーロッパを築いてゆくという約束でもあるのだ。ベルリンの持つ魅力はヨーロッパ大陸の安定化の軸のひとつとなり、ベルリンとヨーロッパは互いに不可欠となるだろう。首都ベルリンは独創的で創造力にあふれ、自由で個性的なヨーロッパの神経中枢のひとつである。ベルリンはヨーロッパ文化の多層構造と豊かさを理解するためにはまさにもってこいの場所なのである。

柏林,从柏林宫展望卢斯特花园(十九世纪钢版雕刻画) / Vista al jardín del deseo / ベルリン市、ベルリンの城から見たルスト・ガルテンの眺め(19世紀の鋼版画)

勃兰登堡门建于一七九一年。从那以后它见证了德国皇帝时代披上盛装的游行队伍，第一次世界大战中它既见证了的凯旋而归的胜利之师，也见证了断羽而回的败军队伍；勃兰登堡门见证了一九一八年的革命斗争；一九三三年一月三十日的星期六火炬游行；见证了苏联红军占领柏林；一九六一年八月十三日柏林墙的建造；也见证了一九八九年十一月九日东西德边境开放后，来自全球各地的年轻人在柏林墙上载歌载舞的欢庆场景；勃兰登堡门还见证了一九八九年人山人海的除夕庆祝活动以及一九九零年十月三日德国统一日成千上万的庆祝人群。

The gate was built in 1791. The gate has witnessed the festive entries into the city in the imperial Period, the victorious, but also the defeated troups of World War I, the revolutionary fights of 1918, the torchlight procession of the SA on January 30, 1933, the occupation of Berlin by the Soviet army, the building of the Wall on August 13, 1961, young people from all over the world dancing on the Wall after its opening on November 9, 1989, and a rambunctious New Year's celebration in the same year, as well as thousands of people on the day of reunification, October 3, 1990.

ブランデンブルク門は、1791年に建造された。それ以来第一次大戦の勝ち誇った軍隊や打ち破られた軍隊、1918年の革命戦、ナチス突撃隊の松明行列(1933年1月30日)、ソ連軍によるベルリン占領、壁構築(1961年8月13日)、壁崩壊(1989年11月9日)後世界中からやって来た何千人もの若者、その年の大晦日の祝い、翌年1990年10月3日ドイツ再統一の日に集まったあふれんばかりの民衆と、現代ドイツの歴史を見守ってきた。

首都柏林, 带有玻璃穹顶的国会大厦 / Reichstag with glass dome / 首都ベルリン、ガラスの円蓋をもつ旧帝国議事堂

将国会大厦建筑物改建成德意志联邦共和国议会举行会议的场所是德国政治中心从波恩迁到柏林的显著标志。城市建筑, 主要是东部地区的大规模重新设计明显表达了柏林对未来经济辐射力的希望。一九九九年四月十九日, 按照诺曼·弗斯特的规划改建的国会大厦被德意志联邦共和国议会正式接受。新国会大厦的标志—玻璃穹顶也对游客开放, 游客可入内参观。

The redesign of the Reichstag building as the place where the Federal government now convenes is an unmistakable symbol of the transition of power in the Republic from Bonn to Berlin. The momentous changes to the city's architecture, especially in the east, are a visible expression of the hopes invested in Berlin's future economic strength and the influence to emanate from it to the surrounding area. On 19th April 1999 the German Bundestag held its inaugural session in the building redesigned by Sir Norman Foster. The glass dome is open to the public.

旧帝国議会の建物が新しい連邦国議会の議事堂に生まれ変わることは、統一ドイツの政治の中心が従来のボンからベルリンへ移行したことのシンボルとしてまことにふさわしい。とりわけ東側地区で公共建築物が集中的に改築されるのを見ると、未来のベルリンの発展に明るい希望が約束されているようだ。ノーマン・フォスター卿の設計により改築された旧帝国議会の建物は、1999年4月19日にドイツ連邦国議会に引き渡された。建物の特徴となっているガラスの円蓋はだれでも中に入って見学することができる。

在国会大厦中德国联邦议会的议会会场 / Plenary assembly, Lower House / 旧帝国議事堂内の連邦議会総会議場

这座国会大厦建筑物又重新获得了一个玻璃穹顶，它不是最初的历史形状，而是二十世纪建筑大师的杰作。这一穹顶能够满足三大功能：为参观者提供了一个平台，使其能够从这里环视柏林；同时穹顶玻璃和钢结构中的一个灯光和通风技术锥形部件能够提供自然光线并有通风功能。从内部照明的透明穹顶成了德意志联邦共和国首都柏林的一个新的标志。

The building again has a glass dome, not, however, in the original historical form but in the architectural style of the late 20th century. The dome has three functions: a viewing platform offers visitors a panorama of Berlin; at the same time a cone-shaped technical feature incorporated into the steel and glass dome construction provides the building with natural light and ventilation. And finally, the internally lit transparent dome is intended to be a new symbol and landmark of the federal capital.

建物には再びガラスの円蓋がつけられたが、もともとあった歴史的な形ではなく、20世紀の建築様式に改められている。円蓋は三つの役目を果たしている。まず第一に見学者が展望台からベルリン市を見渡せるようにすることである。次に、ガラスと鋼鉄で造られた円蓋に取り付けられている通光・通気装置が採光と換気を調節するのである。そして第三に、内側から照明をつけた時に透明な円蓋が首都ベルリンの新しいシンボルとなるのである。

联邦政府部门 / Federal Ministries / 連邦各省

△ Federal Ministry for economics and technology

△ Foreign Office

△ Federal Ministry of the inside

▽ Federal Ministry for traffic, building and housing △ Office of the Federal Chancellor ▽ Dorotheenbloecke – offices of the Lower House

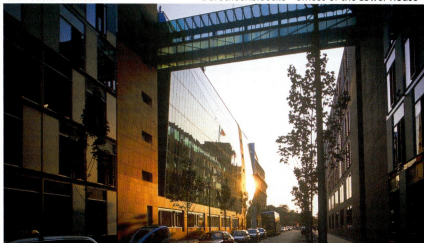

尽管战争造成了许多无法挽回的损失，但柏林依然是一个光华四射的城市。尤其是反抗拿破仑的自由战争后，柏林这一普鲁士首都开始上升为以古典主义为标志的"施普雷河畔的雅典"。宪兵广场上过去的戏剧院中，现在只举办交响音乐会。在两侧德意志教堂和法兰西教堂的拱卫下，每年六、七月间都会在这一戏剧院前举办露天古典音乐节。

Berlin is still a splendid city, despite the fact that so much was irretrievably lost in the war. It was chiefly after the wars of liberation against Napoleon that the Prussian capital and its architecture evolved in classicistic style to become ìAthens on the Spreeî. The former playhouse on the Gendarmenmarkt is now only a venue for concerts. The Classic Open Air Festival takes place each June/July outside the playhouse, flanked on either side by the French and German cathedrals.

ベルリンは大戦で原形の大部分を壊滅的に失ったが、今尚輝き続けている都市である。特にナポレオンに対抗した解放戦争(1813年～15年)後は、このかつてのプロイセン王国の首都は擬古典主義の象徴として「シュプレー河畔のアテネ」と呼ばれるまでになった。ジャンダーメン・マルクト(巡査市場)にある旧演劇場は、今日ではコンサートホールとして使われている。毎年6月と7月になると、左右に双子のようなドイツとフランスの大聖堂が建つこの劇場前広場でクラシックの野外コンサートが開催される。

GENDARMENMARKT / FRIEDRICHSSTRASSE

宪兵广场建于大约一七三五年,这一广场上最古老的建筑物要数建于一七零五年的法兰西弗里德里希城市教堂。一七零八年在它的对面建起了德国教区的教堂。根据弗里德里希大帝的指令,一七八零年至一七八五年间两座教堂都建起了穹形塔楼,并分别被称为法兰西教堂和德意志教堂。这两座教堂都是按照卡尔·冯·巩塔尔德的设计以古典主义风格建造的。一从弗里德里希大街火车站出发,人们可以展望新的、富丽堂皇的弗里德里希大街。弗里德里希大街在柏林历史老城的中心与"菩提树下大街"相交。

The oldest building in the Gendarmenmarkt, a square laid out in 1735, is the French Friedrichstadtkirche (built in 1705). Opposite the church stands the former Kirche of the German congregation, built in 1708. On the orders of Frederick the Great, domed towers designed by Carl von Gontard were added to the east end of both churches between 1780 and 1785. – From Friedrichstrasse station there is a view of the elegant new shopping street of the same name. It is here, in the centre of historic Berlin, that this street crosses the famous "Unter den Linden" boulevard.

1735年整備された広場に建つ最も古い建物は、1705年に建てられたフランスのフリードリッヒシュタット教会だ。1709年にはその向かい側に、ドイツ人教区の教会が建造された。フリードリッヒ大王の下知により、両教会に小円蓋の塔が作られ(1780年から1785年)、フランス大聖堂、ドイツ大聖堂と呼ばれるようになった。カール・フォン・ゴンタードによって擬古典主義様式を取り入れて設計された。この通りは、古い歴史的なベルリンの中心区の真ん中で、「ウンター・デン・リンデン」通りとぶつかる。

弗里德里希大街，拉法亚特精品画廊

德意志民主共和国试图通过建造弗里德里希城文化宫以及一九八七年开张的大饭店让这世界城的林荫大道—弗里德里希大街重新得以振兴。一九八九年东西德统一之前，弗里德里希大街变成了一个巨大的建筑工地。一九八九年后，对这条大街进行了更大规模的建设。无数的宾馆、饭店、出版社以及银行等希望到此安营扎寨，这样今天的弗里德里希大街重新放射出旧日的光彩，游客可有很多高档购物和娱乐消遣的可能性。

Friedrichstrasse, Galeries Lafayette

The GDR tried to bring back the glory of cosmopolitan Friedrichstrasse with buildings like the Friedrichstadt Palace and the Grand Hotel, which opened in 1987. By the time the Wall came down in 1989, Friedrichstrasse had become a huge building site. After '89 building went on even more vigorously. Hotels, restaurants, publishing houses, banks etc. wanted to establish themselves here. Today, all the former glory has returned, with exclusive shops and entertainment offering visitors countless opportunities to enjoy themselves.

フリードリッヒ通り、ラファイエッテ・ギャラリー

旧東ドイツはフリードリッヒシュタット・パラストと1987年に開店したグランドホテルを建てることによって、フリードリッヒ通りを世界的に有名な大通りとして復興させようとした。1989年の大転換の時までフリードリッヒ通りは巨大な建築現場だった。1989年以降、計画中だった建造物が大規模に出現した。いくつものホテル、レストラン、出版社、銀行などがここに置かれ、現在ではフリードリッヒ通りは再び栄光に輝いている。散策や高級店でのショッピングを楽しむためにここを訪れる客は後を絶たない。

弗里德里希城—商业走廊

一座台阶,一座天梯,一座美国拉斯维加斯风格的天梯,它们好像是为了让职业表演行业的明星们能从这里下来,去接受自己爱好者团体的欢呼而特设的。在"二零六号商厦",在弗里德里希大街七十一号,这里也是娱乐消遣的乐园:这里是大型购物表演的热点。弗里德里希大街过去曾是普鲁士皇帝皇宫区的豪华一条街。一八七三年"德国皇帝精品廊"曾在这里开张,德国百货公司文化就是从这里开始一并将在这里重新复兴一没有供客户翻检商品用的廉价商品堆积台,没有季末大甩卖。

Friedrichstadt Passage

A staircase, a celestial ladder in the style of Las Vegas, on which the gods of showbiz could descend to their lesser-mortals fan-clubs. Quartier 206's business is entertainment: a great shopping show. Friedrichstraße was once the Champs Elysées of the royal Prussian Residence. The Emperor's Gallery was opened here in 1873. And this is where department-store culture began in Germany - and is set to continue, in a style that ignores bargain counters and sales, of course.

フリードリッヒシュタット・パサージェ

ラスベガスのショービジネスの神々のために造られたようなスタイルの階段、天の梯子はファンの中に降りて来るかのようだ。フリードリッヒ通り71にある「クォティア206」と言えば、エンターテイメント、つまり盛大なショッピング・ショー。フリードリッヒ通りは、かつてプロイセン王の居城があった華やかな通りで、1873年には「カイザー・ギャラリー」が開かれた。ドイツのデパート文化がここに始まった——目玉商品コーナーやバーゲンセールを呼び物にしない百貨店が再びここに復興してくるだろう。

新的弗里德里希大街 / The new FRIEDRICHSSTRASSE / 新生フリードリッヒ通り

弗里德里希大街是古老的南北交通要道,它从哈勒舍恩门的梅林广场一直通到奥拉宁堡门。在弗里德里希·威廉一世的时代,弗里德里希大街是前往设在圣庙大院旷野中的演兵场的行进大道。威廉二世的时代,军队演练完毕也取道弗里德里希大街回到皇宫。柏林的德国皇帝时代,弗里德里希大街曾是城中首屈一指的商业和娱乐大街。大约一九零零年这里曾有高档宾馆、银行、小歌剧院、歌舞剧宫以及许多其它设施。

Friedrichstrasse is the old north-south axis, running from Mehringplatz by the Halle Gate to Oranienburg Gate. In the time of Frederick William I, Friedrichstrasse was the direct marching route to the parade ground on Tempelhof Feld. Troops continued to use this route from exercise to the castle in the days of William II. In imperial times Friedrichstrasse was the focus of business and entertainment in the city. Around 1900 there were stylish hotels, banks, operetta houses, music halls and much more besides.

フリードリッヒ通りはハレ門のあるメーリンク広場からオラーニエンブルク門まで走るかつての南北幹線道路である。フリードリッヒ・ヴィルヘルム1世の時代にはテンペルホーファー・フェルドの練兵場へ直接通じる行軍用路であった。さらにヴィルヘルム2世の治下でも機動演習地から王宮へ戻る行軍用路として使われた。その後フリードリッヒ通りはベルリンで初めての商業・歓楽街となって栄え、1900年頃には上品なホテルや銀行、オペレッタ劇場やレビュー劇場などが立ち並んだ。

波茨坦广场 / POTSDAMER PLATZ / ポツダム広場

索尼中心论坛

几乎没有其他的大都市能不断把如此众多的文化、科学、商界以及工业巨头吸引到自己身边。他们都被柏林多姿多彩的推动力所感染、所鼓舞,并始终都在为把柏林作为欧洲中心推波助澜。波茨坦广场—这里是柏林城东和城西的接口,现又成了柏林充满活力的城市中心之一。索尼论坛是一个光线充沛、带有顶棚的区域,它是波茨坦广场上的索尼中心的中心。这四千平方米的公共广场为文化盛事、电影、购物以及餐饮业提供了一个令人兴奋的氛围。

Sony Center Forum

There is hardly another capital city that has attracted so many of the big names of culture, science, trade and industry. They were all inspired by the multifarious influences that Berlin exerts as the centre of Europe. Potsdamer Platz, the meeting point of the city's east and west, has once again become the vibrant heart of the city. The forum, a roofed area flooded with light, forms the centre of the Sony Center on Potsdamer Platz. The 4000-square-meter public square has a stimulating atmosphere with cutural events, cinemas, shops and restaurants.

ソニーセンターにあるフォーラム

文化、学術、商工業といった分野の偉大な人々をこれほどまでに惹きつけてやまない都市は他にない。彼らの誰もがベルリンがヨーロッパの中心として及ぼしてきたさまざまな影響からインスピレーションを得てきたのだ。東ベルリン市と西ベルリン市の裂け目であったポツダム広場は、生き生きとしたベルリンの中心に生まれ変わった。光を通す屋根付アレーナとして、フォーラムはポツダム広場にあるソニーセンターのシンボルとも言える。4000平方メートルの広場には、文化イベント、映画、ショッピング、レストランなど人々をワクワクさせる雰囲気が漂っている。

索尼论坛的国王大厅

一九零八年开张的埃斯普拉内达酒店曾是德国皇帝威廉二世时代最豪华的酒店之一。这一酒店曾是国际明星,如查理·卓别林以及葛丽泰·嘉宝等的汇聚点。第二次世界大战时,这一建筑物几乎被完全摧毁。只有国王大厅和早餐厅得以幸存。人们曾花费了惊人的巨额费用将这两个房间移动了大约七十米,并将其整合到索尼论坛新的现代化建筑群中;这一整合为索尼中心增添了一种思乡怀古的现代魅力。

Emperor hall at the Sony-Forum

In the time of the German Emperor William II, the Hotel Esplanade, which opened originally in 1908, was one of the most famous buildings in Berlin. It became the meeting place of international stars such as Charlie Chaplin and Greta Garbo. The building was almost completely destroyed in the Second World War. Only the Imperial Room and the Breakfast Room were preserved. Both rooms were dismantled or transported on air cushions to their new location in the modern Sony complex, about 70 m away from where they originally stood. They add an nostalgic touch to the Sony Centre.

ソニーフォーラムにあるカイザーザール

ドイツ皇帝ヴィルベルム2世の時世、ホテル・エスプラナーデ(1908年開館)は最も優雅なホテルのひとつだった。チャーリー・チャップリンやグレタ・ガルボといった国際的スターが集まる場所になっていった。第二次世界大戦でホテル建造物はほとんどが破壊されてしまったが、わずかにカイザー広間と朝食室が壊れずに残った。この2つの間は、驚くような経費を費やして70メートル先の新しい所在地、近代的な建物群ソニーフォーラムの中へと移された。郷愁的なチャーミングさでこのモダンな建物を一層魅力的にしている。

柏林通讯博物馆 / Museum of Communication / 通信技術博物館

今天的"柏林通讯博物馆"是一八七二年作为全世界第一个邮政博物馆创建的。柏林通讯博物馆的常年展览使人们能够在此体验和了解信息社会的发展和未来前景。博物馆的入口从建筑学上给人留下难忘的影响,机器人在此接待来宾,并要求与客人们进行通讯交流以及互通信息。博物馆以游戏娱乐的方式向来宾提出许多有关历史、现在和未来的问题并有许多非常值得一看的展品供观众参观、欣赏。

The present-day Museum of Communication was founded in 1872 as the first postal museum in the world. Today it houses a permanent exhibition on the development and future of the information society, with state-of-the art hands-on experiences. Visitors are greeted by robots in the architecturally imposing entrance area and encouraged to communicate and participate. For example in games on numerous aspects of the past, present and future. And there are a large number of interesting exhibits.

今日ある「ベルリン通信技術博物館」は1872年世界で最初の郵便博物館として創設された。情報化社会の進歩発展・将来の方向性をわかりやく体験できるようにと、常時展示会を行ってきた。印象的な建築様式をもった博物館入口をはいると、ロボットが来場客を迎えてくれ、コミュニケーション、相互作用を求めてくる。過去、現在、未来に関する質問に対しては、楽しいアトラクションも用意されている。興味深い展示物も広範囲にわたっている。

玛琳·黛德丽广场 / MARLENE-DIETRICH-PLATZ / マレーネ・ディートリッヒ広場

二次世界大战中,波茨坦广场的百分之八十被毁坏;柏林被分割成两半后的四十多年里这里变得荒无人烟。一九八九年柏林墙被推倒后,这里开始建设一个远远超过旧时波茨坦广场的巨大区域。其中的一个广场是以生于一九零一年的著名女演员玛琳·黛德丽命名的。玛琳·黛德丽通过电影"蓝天使"脱颖而出,成为电影明星。三十年代她在美国好莱坞青云直上,一九三九年成为美国女公民。玛琳·黛德丽于一九九二年安葬在柏林。

80 % of the Potsdamer Platz was destroyed in the Second World War, and in the forty-year long bisection of the city it faded away into the desolation of no man's land. When the wall came down in 1989, the city of Berlin started a restoration of the Potsdamer Platz area. A square is named after the famous actress Marlene Dietrich, born in 1901. The film "Der blaue Engel" catapulted her to stardom. In the 1930s she made a career in Hollywood and became a US citizen in 1939. She was buried in Berlin in 1992.

第二次世界大戦のためにポツダム広場はその約80パーセントが崩壊し、東西ベルリンの分裂により40年以上にもわたって人気のない荒廃した土地となってしまった。しかし1989年のベルリンの壁の崩壊後、この広大な土地に建築ラッシュがおとずれ、かつてのポツダム広場をはるかに越えて建築工事が繰り広げられている。ひとつの広場はあの有名な女優マレーネ・ディートリッヒ(1901年生れ)の名にちなんで命名された。映画「青い天使」でフィルムスターとしての名をあげたマレーネは、30年代ハリウッドで活躍し、1939年アメリカ国籍を取得した。1992年ベルリンに没する。

"菩提树下大街"及太子宫 / "UNTER DEN LINDEN", the Crown Prince Palace / クロンプリンツェン宮殿とウンター・デン・リンデン通り

许多天才建筑师对柏林的历史产生了深刻的影响,如巴洛克建筑大师安德里亚·施吕特尔和格奥尔格·温策斯劳斯·冯·克诺伯斯多夫,他们都是洛可可时期最著名的建筑大师。出生在德国新鲁平市的卡尔·弗里德里希·申克尔在创造一定类型的作品方面是无可企及的—新岗亭、宪兵市场上的新剧院、老博物馆或是波茨坦的尼古拉教堂就是其中的一些古典主义范例。战胜拿破仑后日益强盛的普鲁士把申克尔的建筑风格定为国家建筑风格。

Many architects of great genius have shaped Berlin. The baroque master architect Andreas Schlüter and Georg Wenzeslaus von Knobelsdorff of the rococo period are two of the most significant. Yet none of them created such definitive works as Karl Friedrich Schinkel from Neuruppin – textbook examples of classicism like the Neue Wache, the New Playhouse on the Gendarmenmarkt, the Old Museum or Church of St. Nicholas in Potsdam. Schinkel's style became the hallmark of state architecture, as Prussia rose to power after victory over Napoleon.

幾多の天才建築家たちが今あるベルリンの形を造り上げてきたのだ。例えばバロック時代の巨匠アンドレアス・シュリューターやロココ時代の巨匠ゲオルク・ヴェンツェスラウス・フォン・クノーブルスドルフはその中でも特に重要な人物として挙げられる。新衛兵所、巡査市場の新演劇場、旧博物館、あるいはポツダムにあるニコライ教会など擬古典主義の模範例は枚挙に暇がない。シンケルの建築様式はナポレオンに対して勝利をおさめた後、強大になっていくプロイセン王国そのものの代表的様式となった。

望景宫

施普雷路上的望景宫镶嵌在公园景致之中,从一九五九年起,它是德意志联邦共和国总统的官邸。这座一七八五年至一七八六年由米夏埃尔·菲利普·波曼设计建造的望景宫在艺术史上具有很高的价值。这座建筑物虽然设计建造于巴洛克晚期,却已显示了古典主义风格。这种新风格明显可见的佐证是由卡尔·高特哈德·朗汉斯设计的椭圆形宴会厅。这座宫殿是为弗里德里希大帝最小的弟弟奥古斯特·费尔迪南德·冯·普鲁士建造的。一九二八年这座宫殿被收归国有,一九三五年这里曾是民俗博物馆,从一九三八年起这里曾是帝国国宾馆。

BELLEVUE PALACE

Nestled in a park, Bellevue Palace on the Spree has been the official seat of the president of the Ferderal Republic since 1959. The palace, designed in 1785-86 by Michael Philipp Boumann, occupies an interesting place in the history of art. Built at the end of the Baroque period, it already incorporates neoclassical elements. Evidence of this is the oval banquet-hall designed by Carl Gotthard Langhans. The place was built for Frederick the Great's youngest brother. in 1928 it became state property, in 1935 it housed an ethnology museum and in 1938 it was turned into a guest-house of the Reich.

ベルヴュー宮殿

シュプレーヴェークの公園内に建つベルヴュー宮殿は1959年以来連邦大統領の官邸になっている。ミヒャエル・フィリップ・バウマンが1785年から1786年に建てたこの宮殿は、非常に美術史的価値の高いもので、バロック後期に建てられたため、すでに擬古典主義の影響が窺える。カール・ゴットハルト・ラングハンスの設計した楕円形の宴会ホールにまさにこの新しい様式が見られる。もともとはフリードリッヒ大王の一番下の弟にあたるアウグスト・フェルディナンド・フォン・プロイセンのために造られたもので、1928年国家所有になり、1935年には国民博物館として利用された。1938年以降は、帝国の迎賓館として使われるようになった。

宫殿桥, 从桥上展望大教堂 / SCHLOSSBRÜCKE / 城の橋から眺める大聖堂　　柏林大教堂—大门一面 / BERLINER DOM / ベルリン大聖堂、正面入口

十九世纪最著名的德国建筑师卡尔·弗里德里希·申克尔为菩提树下大街的西端设计了建造于一八二二年至一八二四年间的宫殿桥。八个耸立在高大的雕像基座上的白色大理石群雕展示了在女神尼克、密涅瓦、伊里斯以及帕拉斯·雅典娜领导下一个斗士的生活。这座宫殿桥横跨在施普雷河上。这里也是河上游船停泊的地方，游客们可在此登船，凭借柏林丰富的水上航道，环游柏林城。

The western terminus of the boulevard Unter den Linden, the Schlossbrücke built in 1822-1824, was designed by the most important German architect of the 19th century, Karl Friedrich Schinkel. The eight marble groups of statues on high pediments depict the goddesses Nike, Minerva, Iris and Pallas Athene. The bridge spans the River Spree, and here there is a moo-ring-place for the river steamers which cruise along Berlin's numerous waterways, offering visitors interesting sightseeing tours of the city.

1822年から1824年にかけて城の橋を建設したカール・フリードリッヒ・シンケルは、ウンター・デン・リンデン通りの西端に、19世紀の最も重要なドイツ建築を設計した。高い台座の上にある大理石の8つの群像は、女神ニーケ、ミネルヴァ、イーリス、パラスアテーネーの指揮のもと戦った兵士の一生を表している。シュプレー河に架かる城の橋には、河川遊覧船の船着場があり、ベルリンを流れる広範囲な水路を通って一味違った市内観光をすることもできる。

柏林大教堂

柏林大教堂建于一八九四年至一九零五年，是在德国皇帝威廉二世时期，由尤柳斯·拉施道夫规划设计的。柏林大教堂不断被艺术史学家们批评为是一种建筑艺术衰退的表现，直到今天才作为德国皇帝时代的建筑资料在建筑史上占有一席之地。这座按照意大利文艺复兴时期的风格设计的大教堂在二次世界大战中严重受损。一九七四年开始重建。大教堂的内部直到一九九七年才最终竣工。在教堂墓室中存有将近一百具霍恩措伦王室的棺木，其中包括安德里亚·施吕特尔设计的豪华棺木。

BERLIN CATHEDRAL

Sponsored by Emperor Wilhelm II-, Julius Raschdorf was contracted to do the planning. The church was erected between 1894 and 1905. Art historians have called it a decline in achitecture and only recently has it been granted its proper place in the history of architecture as a typical example of building in the Imperial Period. Built in the Italian High Renaissance style, it was heavily damaged in World War II. Reconstruction began in 1974. The crypt contains more than 100 coffins of the Hohenzollern, among them sarcophagi designed by Andreas Schlüter.

ベルリン大聖堂

ベルリン大聖堂は皇帝ヴィルヘルム2世の治世下にユーリウス・ラシュドルフによって設計され、1894年から1905年までかけて完成された。美術史学者からしばしば建築芸術の堕落であると厳しい批判を受けてきたが、今日になってようやく皇帝時代の記念的建築物として建築史上に位置付けられるようになった。イタリア盛期ルネッサンス様式の大聖堂は第二次世界大戦中に著しく破損し、1974年に修復工事が開始された。大聖堂の内部修復は1997年になってようやく完了した。大聖堂の地下納骨堂には約100台のホーエンツォレルン王家の柩が収められており、その中にはアンドレアス・シュリューターがデザインした豪華な柩もある。

在施普雷河畔展望尼古拉区
Nicolai-Viertel near the Spree
シュプレー河沿いのニコライ横町

Senate House, Neptun Fountain

海神喷泉是柏林市于一八八八年送给德国皇帝威廉二世的礼物。它于一八九一年建于宫殿广场。二次世界大战时它被用一道保护墙保护了起来。一九四五年后，海神喷泉被拆掉。拆下来的单一部分一直被保存到一九六九年。莱因侯尔德·贝嘎斯设计创造的这一海神喷泉中央是坐在一个巨大贝壳上的海神。喷泉池的边上是莱茵河女神、易北河女神、威斯瓦河女神以及奥德河女神的雕像。从一九九一年十月一日起，海神喷泉背后的市政厅现在是柏林市政府所在。

The Neptune Fountain was the city's present to Emperor Wilhelm II (1888). It was erected in 1891 opposite the junction of Schlossplatz and Breite Straße. During World War II it was bricked in. After 1945, it was dismanteld and put into storage until its reassembly in 1969 near the church Marienkirche. Designed by Reinhold Begas, it depicts Neptune sitting in a great shell in the centre of fountain. On the edge of the basin female figures symbolise the rivers Rhine, Elbe, Weichsel and Oder. The city hall in the background has been the seat of the Berlin Senate since October 1, 1991.

「海神ネプチューンの噴水」は、ベルリン市が皇帝ヴィルヘルム2世に寄贈した(1888年)もので、1891年には王宮広場に建てられていた。戦時中は石塀で保護されたが、1945年のち撤去された。取り壊された一つ一つの部分は、1969年まで倉庫にしまわれていた。ラインホルト・ベガスによって造られた噴水の中央には、大きな貝殻にネプチューンが座っている。泉水の縁に置かれた女性像は、それぞれライン河、エルベ河、ヴァイクセル河、オーデル河を象徴している。写真奥の市庁舎には1991年10月1日からベルリンの市参事会が置かれている。

尼古拉区的格奥尔格·布劳啤酒酿造厂 / Brewery GeorgBræu at the NIKOLAIVIERTEL / ニコライ横町にあるゲオルクブロイ・ビール醸造所

人们把尼古拉区称为是柏林的摇篮。尼古拉区最早见于一二四四年文字记载中。当时已有尼古拉教堂,它是尼古拉区的标志。人们为了感谢该区的保护神—神圣的尼古劳斯,所以把这一地区命名为尼古拉区。尼古拉教堂是一个具有歌特式建筑风格的厅堂式教堂,它具有杰出的声学效果,所以现在多被用来举办音乐表演,尼古拉教堂的组钟钟乐演奏也非常值得聆听和欣赏。一啤酒酿造厂(见下图)是以神圣的格奥尔格命名的,神圣格奥尔格的雕像就紧贴着尼古拉区。

The Nikolaiviertel, or St Nicholas quarter, is known as the cradle of Berlin. A church dedicated to Saint Nicholas [Nikolaikirche], a local landmark which gave its name to the quarter, was already in existence at this time. St Nicolas is a Gothic hall church with superb acoustics which today houses part of the City Museum. Don't forget to stop and listen to the church's fine carillon. – The brewery in the picture is named after St George, whose statue stands in the neighbourhood.

ニコライ横町はベルリン発祥の地とも言える場所で、史的資料の中に初めてこの名が登場するのは1244年のことである。現在もニコライ横町のシンボルであるニコライ教会は、その当時からあった。この横町の名は、守護聖人ニコラウスに由来する。ゴシック式の教会は素晴らしい音響効果を持ち、今日では博物館の目的にも利用されている。グロッケンシュピールも聴く価値がある。ビール醸造所(写真下)の名前は聖人ゲオルクに由来し、すぐ近くにはこの聖人の像がある。

护城河畔的德国技术博物馆以及高架铁路线, 从这里展望波茨坦广场 / DEUTSCHES TECHNIKMUSEUM, Landwehrkanal / ランドヴェア運河沿いのドイツ技術博物館

在"一号线"高架铁路区段的格莱斯德来埃克站和缪肯布吕克站之间, 耸立着雄伟的德国技术博物馆, 德国技术博物馆还占用了过去安哈尔特运火车站的站区。博物馆的顶上是一架展翅欲飞的C 47"空中列车"型美国军用飞机, 这既是为了吸引人们的视线, 也是为了纪念一九四八年六月二十四日至一九四九年五月十二日柏林危机时期英美向西柏林运送食品和日用必需品所架起的空中桥梁。当年这架飞机负责为柏林提供日用必需品, 并因此被昵称为"葡萄干轰炸机"。

Along the elevated section of the number 1 line, between Gleisdreieck and Möckern Bridge Stations, is the imposing building of the German Museum of Technology, incorporated into which is the area of the former Anhalter Station with a whole range of historical old locomotives. As an eye-catcher, and in memory of the Berlin Airlift from 24th June 1948 to 12th May 1949, an American military plane, the C 47 Skytrain, hovers above the roof of the museum. Planes of this type supplied Berlin with everyday essentials and so were nicknamed "Rosinenbomber" (currant bombers).

「一番路線」の高架鉄道路線区のグライスドライエック駅とミュケルンブリュッケ駅の間には威風堂々としたドイツ技術博物館が建っている。かつてのアンハルト駅の作業敷地も含んでいる。博物館の屋根の上には、1948年6月24日から1949年5月12日まで行われたベルリン空輸を記念して、アメリカ空軍機C47「スカイトレイン」が浮かんでおり、誰もが目を引かれる。当時この空軍機は日々必要な物資をベルリンの街に補給したことで、「ロジーネンボンベ(干し葡萄の爆弾)」と呼ばれるようになった。

OBERBAUMBRÜCKE, S-Bahn Linie No. 1 / 一番路線とオーバーバウム橋

奥伯鲍姆桥是以"勃兰登堡省的砖结构哥特式建筑风格"设计建造的。这一高架铁路区段通过音乐剧"一号线"闻名四方。一九九零年前,这一区域的施普雷河曾是东西柏林之间的边界线。东西柏林重新统一前,奥伯鲍姆桥上的地铁区段一直被停止使用。奥伯鲍姆桥的左边与"华沙大街"火车站相连。一作为柏林市中心的东大门,业主和建筑师们看好这里良好的地理位置和便利的交通环境,在此建起了令人瞩目的办公和商业大楼—"特里亚斯大楼"。

The Oberbaum Bridge was built in the so-called Brick Gothic style. The musical "Linie 1" has made the elevated section famous. The line goes all the way to the western part of Berlin. Up to 1990 the Spree, including the section spanned by the Oberbaum Bridge, was the boundary between East and West Berlin, and this stretch of the line was therefore closed. Adjacent to the bridge on the left is Warsaw Street Station. – The architects who designed the imposing office building in the strategically important location between the River Spree, the S-Bahn and the main traffic.

オーバーバウム橋は「メルキッシュ風の煉瓦」を使ったゴシック様式の橋である。ミュージカル「一番路線」のお陰で、この高架鉄道路線は有名になった。1990年以前のこの地区では、シュプレー河が東西ベルリンの境界線になっていた。オーバーバウム橋までで地下鉄は遮断された。橋の左側で「ワルシャワ通り」駅と接続している。交通の便がよい「トリアス」と呼ばれるオフィスや会社が集中する一画は、その持ち主、建築家にベルリン中心に向かう東の入口と思われている。

△ Oberbaum Bridge

△ Trias Office Buildings

▽ ROMANTIK AT THE METRO-LINIE 1, STATION WARSCHAUERSTRASSE

▽ Station Jannowitz Bridge, Trias Building

42 　一九八九年前的"柏林墙"以及边界通道"查理检查站" / „Mauer" before 1989, „Checkpoint Charlie" / 1989年ドイツ再統一前の壁、検問所「チェック・ポイント・チャーリー」

这里,在波茨坦广场,在过去竖立着柏林墙的地方,在过去东西柏林的边界所在,柏林死去的心脏近年又得以复苏,并成了二十一世纪新的、生气勃勃的、喧哗的中心。一个神话在这里有了素材和构思。作为史无前例的实验,这里在短短几年中建起了一座大城市。普通情况下这样一座城市的建设既使不需要几个世纪,也要几十年。这里把居住和工作相提并重地混合在一起,商业和文化、政治生活和私人生活生机勃勃、相得益彰。

Potsdamer Platz, is the dead heart of Berlin where once the Wall stood, the border between East and West Berlin, is being resuscitated as the pulsating, whirlwind centre of the 21st century. A myth is being reborn, restructured, for here a section of a great capital city is being created as an experiment that is without historical precedent. In the course of only a few years there will emerge here something that usually takes decades, if not centuries, to develop – a balanced mixture of living and working areas, an association of commerce and culture, the political and the private.

かつて壁が立っていたこのポツダム広場は、東ベルリンと西ベルリンとの境だった。この分裂の期間、ここはベルリンの止まったままの心臓であったが、21世紀には再び脈を打ち、躍動する市の中心地として新しく生まれ変わった。ここで神話は新しい形を取る。歴史上類を見ない方法で、この大都市の一部分は実験的な場所となるのだ。数百年とは言わないまでも、普通数十年かかることがここでは数年以内に、実現しようとしている。同じくらいの数の住居とオフィスが入り混じり、商業と文化が、また政治と私生活が共に手を携えている。

ORIGINAL BERLIN WALL, the "East-Side Gallery", Mühlenstraße

在奥伯鲍姆桥旁,沿着缪伦大街人们可以找到一千三百多米迄今尚存部分中最长的柏林墙残迹—"东边画廊"。一九八九年后,来自全世界的一百多名涂鸦艺术家把德国重新统一前人们无法企及的柏林墙东面变成了一件艺术品。由此,他们在新时代赋予了柏林墙一幅新面目。人们可通过华沙大街的地铁和轻轨铁路车站前往参观"东边画廊"。当年在奥伯鲍姆桥旁曾有一个东西柏林的边界通道。

Close to the Oberbaum Bridge, along Mühlenstraße, is the longest section of the Berlin Wall, the East-Side-Gallery, on Mühlen Str.: This is the longest stretch of the Wall in one piece, 1300 meters long. The painters who worked on this open-air gallery deserve our gratitude for the fact that this original part of the Wall was placed under official heritage protection, and that it is still so well preserved. Nothing has been exchanged here: each part is still standing at its original place. Absolutely authentic evidence of history in our time – history you can reach out and touch.

オーバーバウム橋近くのミューレン通りに沿って、「イーストサイド・ギャラリー」と呼ばれる現存するうちで最も長い1300メートルのベルリンの壁がある。1989年の壁崩壊以来世界中からやってきたグラフィティ・アーティストたちが、それまでは手の届かなかった東側の壁面を芸術作品へと作り変えていった。こうして壁は、新しい時代に新しい顔を持つようになった。最寄の駅は、Sバーンと地下鉄Uバーンの「ワルシャワ通り」駅。オーバーバウム橋には、かつて東ベルリンと西ベルリンを繋ぐ検問所があった。

Berlin Arena at the Prenzlauer Berg

The Berlin Arena (formerly Velodrom) is not only one of the largest all-purpose arenas in Europe, but also provides a striking setting for exceptional events of every kind. It is situated in the centre of the Europa Sport Park in the Prenzlauer Berg district, near the city centre, and has been carefully incorporated into a residential area. With its spectacular design, it makes an imposing sight, for it resembles a space ship about to land. This impression is created by the gigantic steel roof, which seems to defy gravity by floating at a height of thirteen metres above the stadium.

柏林犹太教堂

柏林的新犹太教堂落成于一八六六年，它拥有三千多个座席，当时由于自由犹太人的人数增加，所以需要一个自己的犹太教堂。摩尔人风格的设计符合当时的时代口味。这一建筑物体现了犹太教区的自我意识。新犹太教堂拥有管风琴和合唱队。女子廊台拥有一千个位置。在一九三八年纳粹分子大肆攻击、屠杀犹太人的"水晶之夜"，由于一个警察分局警长勇敢地站了出来，柏林的新犹太教堂有幸没有遭到破坏，但它稍后还是没有逃脱遭炸弹损毁的厄运。

BERLIN SYNAGOGUE

The New Synagogue, which holds a congregation of over 3000, was consecrated in 1866 after the local population of liberal Jews had increased so considerably that they required their own place of worship. The design, in Moorish style, is typical of this period, and its general aspect is an expression of the former self confidence of the Jewish community. The New Synagogue had an organ and a choir, and the women's balcony could seat 1000. The building escaped destruction in the pogrom of November 1938 through the courageous intervention of a police inspector.

ベルリンのシナゴーグ

1866年3千人を収容できる新しいユダヤ教会堂の献堂式が執り行われた。その後リベラルなユダヤ人の数が急増し、別のシナゴーグが必要になった。ムーア式を用いた設計は、時代の趣味に合ったものとなり、教会建物はまさにユダヤ人共同体の自意識を表現していた。新しいシナゴーグにはオルガンが置かれ、聖歌隊ができた。女性用聖歌隊席は1000席を数えた。1938年「水晶の夜」事件の際に、このシナゴーグは勇敢な警察署長の活躍で破壊されずにすんだが、その後結局爆撃により破壊された。

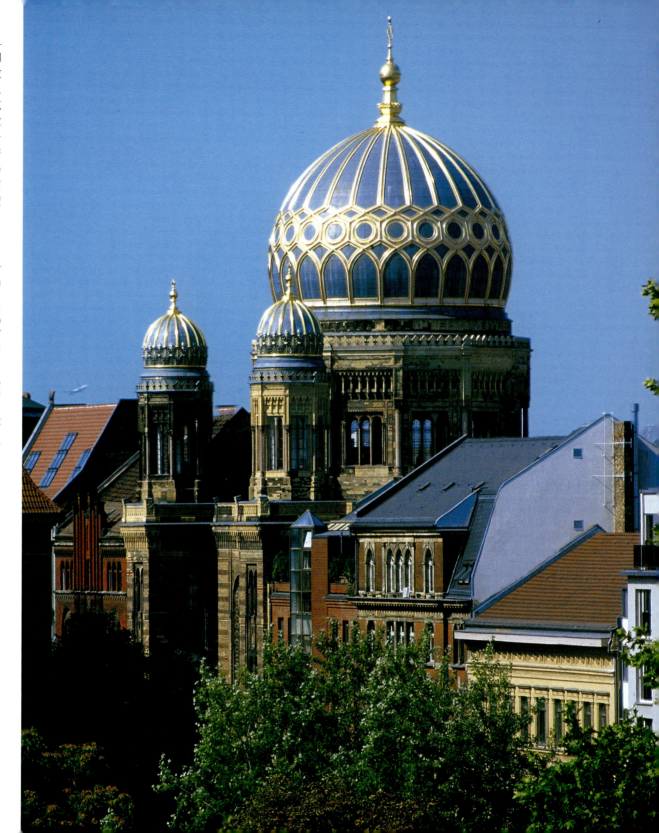

GARDEN OF DESIRE AND THE MUSEUMSISLAND

弗里德里希·威廉四世决定把老博物馆后的区域用来建造其它艺术和科学大楼后,按照弗里德里希·奥古斯特·施蒂勒的设计,一八四三年至一八五七年间建起了新的博物馆。展室内展示的是埃及收藏品。新博物馆就像一座科林斯神庙建造在一个高大的基座上。在老国家美术馆露天台阶的基座上,在入口上方,耸立着创始人弗里德里希·威廉四世的骑马立像。

After Friedrich Wilhelm IV had designated the land behind the museum for the erection of further buildings for the arts and sciences, the „Neues Museum" was built in 1843-1857 to plans by Friedrich August Stüler. Today, the showrooms contain the Egyptian collection. The desire to exhibit contemporary art led to the building of a national gallery. The building rests on a high plinth, akin to a Corinthian temple. On the landing of the outside staircase, above the entrance, stands the statue of its sponsor Friedrich Wilhelm IV, on horseback.

フリードリッヒ・ヴィルヘルム4世は、旧博物館の裏地を芸術・学術のための建築物建設用地に決定した。その決定後、1843年から1857年にかけてフリードリッヒ・アウグスト・シュテューラーが設計を手がけた新しい博物館が建てられた。展示場にはエジプトの収集品が置かれている。コリントの寺院に見られるように高台台石を基礎にして建設された。旧国立美術館の屋外階段の台座、ちょうど入口上には、創立者フリードリッヒ・ヴィルヘルム4世の騎馬像が立っている。

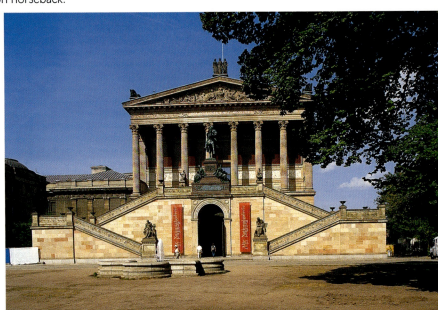

△ The Old Museum at the garden of desire ▽ △ The Old National Galerie ▽ The Pergamon Museum

博物馆岛上的佩加蒙博物馆 / PERGAMON-MUSEUM AT THE MUSEUMSISLAND / ペルガモン博物館と博物館島

博物馆岛躺在老柏林施普雷河的怀抱。佩加蒙博物馆建于一九一二年至一九三零年间,是为收藏古董收藏品、伊斯兰收藏品以及东亚收藏品而建的。佩加蒙博物馆的古董收藏品是世界上最重要的藏品。收藏品的中心是建于公元前一百八十年至一百六十年间的佩加蒙祭坛西侧,这座祭坛是为了纪念雅典娜和宙斯而建的。其它的珍贵藏品还包括大约公元一百二十年后的米莱托市场大门以及西亚博物馆部分的伊斯塔门。

Museum Island, located between two branches of the Spree, is rounded off by the Pergamon Museum, built between 1912 and 1930, with its classical, Islamic and east Asian collections. The classical collection is among the finest in the world. Its centrepiece is the west part of the altar of Pergamon, erected in 180-160 B.C. and dedicated to Athena and Zeus. Other highlights are the market gate of Milet, about 120 A.C., and the Ishtar-Gate in the museum of Asia Minor.

シュプレー河の中洲にある博物館島は、1912年から30年に建てられたペルガモン博物館が加わったことで完成した。世界有数の古代コレクションに加えてイスラムや東アジアのコレクションを誇るペルガモン博物館の最大の展示物は、紀元前180年から160年に建てられ、アテナ神とゼウス神に献じられたというペルガモン祭壇の西側部である。さらにミレト市の門(紀元後120年頃)、西南アジア展示場にあるイシュタル門が見物だ。

▽ The Babylon Istar Gate

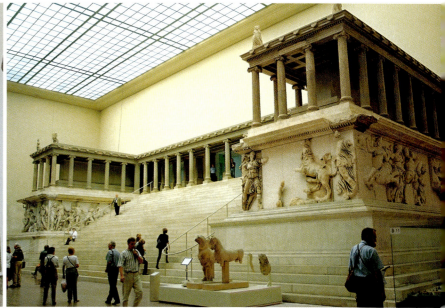
△ The Pergamon-Altar

48 欧洲最大的歌舞剧剧院 / Europe's largest revue theatre / ヨーロッパ最大のレヴュー劇場

在柏林中心,弗里德里希大街旁耸立着欧洲最大的歌舞剧剧院:弗里德里希城文化宫。这独具一格的舞台表演就象勃兰登堡门和无线电塔一样,也是柏林的城市特色之一。每天晚上,柏林本地的居民和游客一起蜂拥到弗里德里希城文化宫中,深深地沉醉到歌舞剧迷人的世界中。美丽的大腿让您看个饱:弗里德里希城文化宫中,成排年轻女演员的精彩表演已经成了舞蹈艺术中不可缺少的保留节目,也是每出歌舞剧的高潮所在。每天晚上,柏林年轻的女演员都会博得观众自发的喝彩和欢呼。

On Friedrichstrasse, in the middle of Berlin, there is Europe's largest revue theatre: the Friedrichstadtpalace. The shows at this unique venue are just as much part of the city's flair as the Brandenburg Gate or the TV tower. Berliners and visitors to Berlin flock to the palace night after night to be transported into the magical world of revue. Lovely legs in abundance: the girls' line-up at the Friedrichstadtpalace is a choreographic must and the climax of each revue. Night after night the Berlin girls are rewarded with storms of enthusiastic applause.

ベルリン中心街のフリードリッヒ通りにはヨーロッパ最大のレヴュー劇場、フリードリッヒシュタット・パラストがある。ブランデンブルク門やテレビ塔がベルリンのシンボルであるように、ここの舞台で繰り広げられる素晴しいショーはベルリンの名物となっている。毎晩のようにベルリン市民と観光客がつめかけ、レヴューの魅惑的な世界の完全な虜となっている。一直線に並ぶ踊り子たち、ほれぼれするような脚線美、見事な振り付け、どこをとってもトップクラスのこのレヴューは絶対に見逃せない。ベルリン・ガール・ダンサーズは今夜も沸き立つ観客の喝采をあびている。

欧洲最大的歌舞剧剧院 / Europe's largest revue theatre / ヨーロッパ最大のレヴュー劇場

除了作为歌舞剧剧院的弗里德里希城文化宫外，柏林还有作为杂艺剧院的、传统的"冬日暖房"以及许多小舞台。对每种口味的观众，柏林都能满足他们的要求；柏林拥有大量对文化充满兴趣的观众。柏林拥有三大歌剧院：菩提树下大街上的国家歌剧院、滑稽歌剧院以及德国歌剧院。柏林拥有几乎五十个舞台，上演范围广博、多姿多彩的戏剧场景，所以人们可在古典戏剧、现代戏剧、街头戏剧以及小型舞台表演之间任意选择。

Besides the Friedrichstadtpalace revue theatre, Berlin has the traditional Winter Garden variety theatre and many other small cabarets as well. There is something for every taste, and a large potential audience; Berlin is a city of great cultural awareness. There are three large opera houses, the State Opera Unter den Linden, the Comic Opera and the German Opera. The theatre scene is both varied and extensive with 50 good theatres and a broad choice of classical, modern and light entertainment productions.

ベルリンで有名なレヴュー劇場としては、フリードリッヒシュタット・パラストの他には「ヴィンター・ガルテン」が昔からある。ここはヴァリエテ劇場であると同時に、様々な小さな出し物を見せることで知られている。ベルリンは芸術に深い関心を持つ観客に、それぞれの趣向にあった催しを提供している。そのために、大きなオペラ劇場が3つある。ウンター・デン・リンデン通りの国立オペラ劇場、コーミッシェ・オペラ劇場、ドイツ・オペラ劇場である。演劇場は50館以上もあり、それぞれ大規模で個性にあふれた舞台をもち、古典、モダン、大衆向きなど、様々なジャンルの演劇が鑑賞できる。

胜利柱 "六月十七日大街"

让我们的目光随着巴洛克式轴心从柏林市中心眺望夏洛滕堡。作为菩提树下大街的继续,"六月十七日大街"把规模巨大的蒂尔加藤公园切成了两半。"巨星"也在巴洛克时代落于此处,从一九三八年起,胜利柱就高高地矗立在此。规模宏大的蒂尔加藤公园过去是勃兰登堡选帝侯的猎区。弗里德里希大帝执政时蒂尔加藤成了向公众开放的公园。彼得·约瑟夫·伦纳对公园进行了规划设计,设置了小路、流水及小岛,这一公园设计一直保留到一九四五年。

STATUE OF VICTORY

The Baroque axis guides the onlooker´s view from Berlin's inner city towards Charlottenburg. A continuation of the boulevard Unter den Linden, the street "Straße des 17. Juni" cuts the park "Großer Tiergarten" in half. The "Großer Stern", since 1938 the site of the Siegessäule, also dates back to the time of the Baroque. The "großer Tiergarten" used to be the hunting grounds of the electors of Brandenburg. In the time of Frederick the Great the area was transformed into a park for the people. It owes the from in which it existed until 1945, with its paths, canals and islands, to Peter Joseph Lenné.

戦勝記念塔

この眺めは、ベルリン市街区からシャルロッテンブルクへと続くバロックの枢軸を示している。「ウンター・デン・リンデン通り」の続きとなる「6月17日通り」は広大なティーアガルテンを横切っている。「グローサー・シュテルン(偉大な星)」もバロック時代のものであり、1938年以来そこに戦勝記念塔が建っている。かつては広大な森林地帯であったティアーガルテンはブランデンブルク選帝侯の狩猟場であった。フリードリッヒ大王の時代に、一般の公園として利用されるようになった。ペーター・ヨゼフ・レネは小道、小川、島を取り入れて造園した。その形は1945年まで存在していた。

柏林大型街庆—爱的游行和文化狂欢节 / Street-Festivals - Love Parade and Carnival of the Culture / ストリート祭り—ラブ・パレードとカルチャー・カーニヴァル

最初唱片骑士莫特博士请了一百五十位宾客举办了一个生日庆祝。年复一年,这一庆祝活动变成了世界上最大的庆祝聚会。富于想象、经常略微化妆的技术音乐爱好者游行穿过柏林。现在世界上到处都有"爱的游行",柏林也许明年又会举办。—作为外国人人数最多的城市,作为国际注目的德国中心,作为世界城市,柏林通过文化狂欢节在多元文化问题以及多种宗教和睦生活方面展示了宽容和开放的态度。

Over the years DJ Dr. Motte´s birthday celebration with 150 guests has growne into the largest parts in the world. Scantilly dressed the techno fans pulled by Berlin. Everywhere in the world there are in the meantime "Love Parades", in Berlin perhaps again next year. – Berlin, as Germany's new capital, is now a metropolis that is a focus of international interest. It is also the city with the highest proportion of foreigners in Germany. In the annual carnival, Berlin demonstrates tolerance and openness for the multitude of cultures and religions, promoting peace and understanding among the groups who coexist here.

150人の招待客を呼んだDJ Dr.モッテの誕生日パーティーが年を重ねて世界で最も大きなパーティーになった。奇想天外な、身軽な服装をしたテクノ狂がベルリンの街を練り歩く。いまや"ラブ・パレード"は世界中に見られる。おそらく翌年もベルリンで行われることだろう。ベルリンは、国内で外国人が最も多い街、国際的な関心が集まるドイツの中心、そして世界都市である。平和な共存をめざし、多種多様な文化・宗教を相互に理解するのに必要な寛容さと開放性をこのカーニヴァルを通して実際に示威している。

◁ LOVE PARADE, Street of the 17th June

Carnival of the Cultures – each June ▽

View from the Bahnhof Zoo / ツォー駅からの眺め

柏林是世界上很少几个拥有两个动物园的城市之一。历史性的老动物园在柏林中心,在动物园火车站旁。新的动物园于一九五五年在柏林弗里德里希斯菲尔德建成开放。历史上的老动物园于一八四四年对外开放,当时柏林市的城市边界还没有划定。早在一八四一年就在亚历山大·冯·洪堡以及彼得·约瑟夫·伦纳的参与下开始将这一老动物园与整个园林一起的设计建造了。它是世界上动物种类最丰富的动物园,放养和笼养动物将近一万两千只。

Berlin is one of the few cities in the world with two zoological gardens. The new zoo, the "Tierpark Berlin", opened its gates in Friedrichsfelde in 1955. The historical zoo is in the centre, opposite to the station of the same name near the Kaiser-Wilhelm Gedächtniskirche. It opened in 1844, at that time only "close to" but not "in" Berlin. The complex was begun as early as 1841 with the help of Alexander von Humboldt and the landscape architect Peter Joseph Lenné. Today it is the zoo with the greatest number of animal species world-wide. Almost 12,000 animals live in its enclosures and houses.

ベルリン市は、2つの動物園を有する世界でも数少ない街のひとつだ。歴史的な動物園は同名のツォー駅のすぐ近くにある。新しいベルリン・ティアーパークは1955年フリードリッヒフェルデに開園された。古い動物園はベルリン市の境界線が置かれる以前1844年に開園されている。1841年すでにアレキサンダー・フォン・フンボルトとペーター・ヨゼフ・レネーの協力のもと、施設の建造が始まった。世界的に見ても動物の種類がかなり多く、屋外・屋内の檻にはほぼ12000匹の動物がいる。

△ Elefant-Gate – Zoo Entrance ▽ Hippo called: Knautscke △ Brown Bear - Berlins heraldic animal ▽ Elefant-Parade

△ 图赫尔咖啡餐馆及沙龙书店
Café-Restaurant TUCHER
サロン書籍店を持つカフェ・レストラン「トゥヒャー」
▽ 了剧院露天平台咖啡店,当年的公主宫建筑物中
Opera Cafe at the Princess Palais
プリンツェシネン宮殿の中にあるテラスカフェ

夜晚沙龙 "世界小灯笼"
The Night-Saloon "The little latern of the world"
居酒屋「ディ・クライネ・ヴェルトラテルネ」
"常人代理" 饭店位于造船工大街附近
Schiffbauer Damm, local "Ständige Vertretung"
レストラン「シュテンディゲ・フェアトレトゥング」

漫步寻诣
A stroll roun
散步

柏林饭店
Berlins restaurants
ベルリンレストラン街

△ "里肯巴克斯"—音乐饭店是柏林威默尔斯多夫区的一家饭店
　"Rieckenbacker's"-Music Inn, in Berlin-Wilmersdorf
　ヴィルマースドルフにある「リーケンベイカース」ミュージック・イン

▽ 柏林施潘道区，施潘道啤酒酿造厂就在老城区中
　Berlin-Spandau, the Spandau brewery
　シュパンダウ地区のシュパンダウ・ビール醸造所

△ 选帝侯大街上的饭店
　Restaurant at the Kurfürstendamm
　クアフュステンダムにあるレストラン

▽ 历史上施潘道要塞的拱顶地窖中
　Vault of the Spandau fortress
　シュパンダウ地区にある歴史的要塞

除了新的柏林市中心、步行街—菩提树下大街、弗里德里希大街以及波茨坦广场区之外,西柏林城市中心选帝侯大街旁的夏洛滕堡区新建的"新克兰茨勒之角大楼"为柏林的城市建筑增添了新的特色。图中人们可见威廉皇帝纪念教堂、新克兰茨勒之角大楼以及六公里之遥矗立在亚历山大广场上的电视塔。

The New Kranzler Corner Complex was constructed on the Kurfürstendamm in the Charlottenburg district of West Berlin, as a pendant to the new focal points of the city, Unter den Linden, Friedrichstrasse and Potsdamer Platz. In the picture you can see the Emperor William Memorial Church, beyond it the new Kranzler Corner, and six kilometres further away, the TV tower on Alexander Square.

新しい街の中心、ブラブラと歩くにふさわしいウンター・デン・リンデン通り、フリードリッヒ通り、ポツダム広場周辺と並んで、西ベルリンの中心区シャルロッテンブルクのクアフュステンダムに「クランツラー・エック・コンプレックス」と呼ばれる新しい建造物群が建ち、ベルリン市の建築にひとつのアクセントを添えた。写真に見えるのは、カイザー・ヴィルヘルム記念教会、新しいカンツラー・エック、6キロメートル離れたアレキサンダー広場に建つテレビ塔。

Emperor William Memorial Church, princely frieze

The Emperor William Memorial Church on Kurfürstendamm, consecrated by Emperor William II in 1895, was destroyed in the Second World War, and the ruins were left standing as a warning to future generations. The great vaulted mosaic with its princely frieze was largely preserved. The splendid mosaics are still a valuable cultural treasure. the history of the Kurfürstendamm dates back to the 16th century. It is closely connected to the building of the hunting seat of Grunewald.In order to reach it from the Berlin palace, a road was required.

要从柏林宫去古纳森林必须有条路。随着时间的推移，这条路逐渐发展成了世界最著名的大街之一——选帝侯大街。这条大街是一八八三年和一八八六年间根据帝国首相奥托·冯·俾斯麦的倡议扩建的。上世纪末，这里还开始了繁复的出租房屋的建造，这些建筑物只有很少部分保存至今。选帝侯大街的黄金时代要数二十年代，当时这里有大约一百家咖啡店和饭店。

This road eventually envolved into one of the most-famous streets in the world. Its construction in 1883-1886 was initiated by the chancellor of the Reich, Otto von Bismarck. The construction of costly residential buildings also began towards the end of the last century. Only a few have remained. The heyday of the boulevard was the Twenties, when about 100 cafés and restaurants lined the street. Many scientists, authors and artists lived at the "Ku-Damm".

ベルリンの宮殿からグリューネヴァルトに至るには、一本の道が必要だった。この一本の道が時代を経るに従って発展し、世界でもっとも有名な大通りの一つ、クアフステンダムとなった。この道路の拡張は1883年から1886年の間に帝国宰相オットー・フォン・ビスマルクの指揮下に行われた。19世紀末頃からは賃借家屋の建築も始まったが、その多くは現在残っていない。大衆劇場の全盛期は20年代で、100軒近くのレストラン、カフェが軒を並べていた。

夏洛滕堡宫

夏洛滕堡宫被旅游者和柏林人珍视为富有魅力的巴洛克建筑,它建于一六九五年到一七九一年间。宫殿的主建筑以及一直延伸五百多米的厢房建筑上都有塔楼,由此构成的丰富多彩的宫殿设施特别受人青睐。夏洛滕堡宫开始时一切都十分简朴。它是按照阿诺尔德·内林的设计于一六九五年到一六九九年间为女选帝侯索菲·夏洛腾建造的一坐行宫。一七零一年选帝侯弗里德里希三世加冕登基成为普鲁士皇帝后,开始在这里大兴土木并把夏洛滕堡宫建成了一座真正的宫殿。

CHARLOTTENBURG PALACE

Built in 1695-1791, the Baroque splendor of Charlottenburg Palace attracts Berliners and tourists alike. Visitors beholding the central building with its tower and adjacent wings are generally struck by the expanse of the palace buildings extending to a length of 550 m. The beginnings, however, were quite modest. In 1695-1699, a small summer castle was built for Electoress Sophie Charlotte according to plans of Arnold Nehring. When Elector Friedrich III was crowned King of Prussia in 1701, builders were briskly put to work at the palace again.

シャルロッテンブルク宮殿

シャルロッテンブルク宮殿(1695年-1791年)は、観光客にはもちろんベルリンっ子にも愛されている魅力的なバロック建築である。塔とその両側に続く翼を持った宮殿は550メートル以上にも広がり、訪れる人を魅了してやまない。しかし、その建設のはじまりは控えめなものだった。選帝侯妃ゾフィー・シャルロッテのために建設されたルスト・ガルテンと呼ばれる夏の離宮が、アーノルト・ネーリングの設計に従って1695年から1699年にかけて出来上がった。1701年選帝侯がフリードリッヒ3世としてプロイセン王の戴冠を受けたことをきっかけに、城の建築は活発に進展するようになった。

60/61

CHARLOTTENBURG CASTLE, Porcelain Cabinet

The manufacture of Berlin porcelain began in the reign of Frederick the Great. The photo shows the porcelain cabinet, a gem in Charlottenburg Castle. In the castle's belvedere there is also a fine collection of Berlin porcelain, with some exceptional exhibits.

埃及博物馆, 埃及美女诺弗莱泰特半身像

夏洛滕堡宫对面是一八五一年到一八五九年间由弗里德里希·奥古斯特·施蒂勒设计建造的当年"近卫军"的兵营。埃及博物馆就建在当年"近卫军"兵营的东营房, 这里珍藏着著名的、用石灰岩制成的埃及美女诺弗莱泰特半身像。

EGYPTIAN MUSEUM, Nefertiti

Across from the palace, the former barracks of the guard are preserved, built in 1851-1859 by Friedrich August Stüler. The building to the east houses the Egyptian museum with its world-famous limestone bust of Nefertiti.

エジプト博物館、王妃ネフェルティティ

エジプト博物館、王妃ネフェルティティの胸像宮殿の向い側にはフリードリッヒ・アウグスト・シュテューラーが1851年から59年にかけて建てたプロイセンの近衛騎兵連隊の兵舎があった。東側の建物はエジプト博物館となっており、石灰石でできた、世界的に有名なエジプト王妃ネフェルティティの胸像がある。

西部戏剧院和海豚宫 / Theater des Westens and the Delphi dance palace / 西の劇場(テアター・デス・ヴェステンス)とデルフィ宮殿

柏林夏洛滕堡的"西部戏院"早年上演的是今天以"音乐剧"闻名的歌剧。剧院大楼和相邻的建筑物构成了对柏林来说非常典型的多种建筑风格的混合。剧院的左边是富有传奇色彩的海豚宫,这座海豚宫在二次世界大战中奇迹般地未遭毁坏。作为保留着战前迷人风姿的舞蹈宫,在进行高水准电影的首映式以及星期天上演"再弹一遍"时,常会勾起观众缕缕思乡怀古之情。

The Theatre of the West in the Charlottenburg district of Berlin used to be the venue of operas, but is now known for its musical productions. To the left of the theatre stands the legendary Delphi dance palace, which by some miracle was spared destruction in the Second World War. This glamorous building dates from the late 1920s and now provides a nostalgic setting for highbrow cinema and 'Play-It-Again' on Sundays.

ベルリン・シャルロッテンブルクにある「西の劇場」は以前オペラが上演されたが、今日ではミュージカル・シアターとして知られている。劇場そのものと隣接する建物はベルリンにふさわしく多くの様式を取り入れて造られている。劇場左側には奇跡的にも第二次世界大戦の被害を免れたデルフィ宮殿が建っている。戦前から魅力的なダンスホールとして、映画のプレミアショーや日曜日の「プレイ・イット・アゲイン」のためにノスタルジーな気分を作った。

路德维希·埃尔哈德商务大楼及柏林证券交易所 / LUDWIG-ERHARD-HAUS and Berlin Stock Exchange / ベルリン商工会議所の入ったルートヴィッヒ・エアハルト・ハウス

路德维希·埃尔哈德商务大楼是柏林证券交易所、柏林工商协会以及许多工商机构的办公场所。楼中每个对公众开放的空间都经过精心设计,使其确实能够适宜举行社会活动,如:展览、时装表演、迎来送往以及举行会议和大会。康德和哈登贝格正厅顶高三十六米,使人能够放眼柏林的天空。在玻璃环境中一百米长的法萨能通道能够举办最多五百人参加的社交聚会式晚宴。

The Ludwig Erhard building houses the Berlin Stock Exchange and other commercial and industrial institutions. Every public room has been designed so that public events really can take place here; exhibitions, fashion shows, receptions, conferences and conventions. The Kant Atrium and Hardenberg Atrium, both with ceilings 36 metres high, afford a view of the skies over Berlin. The glass-fronted Fasanenpassage [Pheasant Passage] is an elegant venue for gala dinners.

ルートヴィッヒ・エアハルト・ハウスには、ベルリン証券取引所や商工会議所、商工業関係の諸機関が入っている。公共の場所は、実際公的目的、例えば展示、ファッションショー、レセプション、ミーティング、会議などに使用できるよう設備が整っている。高さ36メートルの天井を誇るカント・ハルデベルグ・アトリウムからは、ベルリンの空を見渡すことできる。100メートルに及ぶガラス張りのファザーネンパサージェ(雉のアーケード)では、500席まで用意できるガラ・ディナーパーティーが開催される。

柏林无线电塔   ICC ▷

被称为"长长的瘦高个"的无线电塔是柏林的标志之一。它是一九二四年至一九二六年间按照海因里希·施特劳梅尔的规划为第三届德国无线电展建造的。柏林是无线电广播的摇篮。第一次无线电节目是一九二三年十月二十三日由柏林波茨坦大街上的弗克斯大楼（Voxhaus）播放的。—柏林博览会不仅负责十六万平方米展区的博览会展览，而且还负责经营欧洲最大的会议中心—"柏林国际会议中心（简称ICC）"。

RADIO TOWER   ICC/Radio Tower ▷

Another landmark of Berlin is a radio tower, the Funkturm. It was built on 1924-1926 for the 3rd German Radio Exhibition, to plans by Heinrich Straumer. The cradle of radio stood in Berlin. On October 23, 1923, the first radio broadcast in Germany originated from the Voxhaus at Potsdamer Straße 14. – The Berlin trade fair administration is not only responsible for 160,000 square metres of exhibition grounds, but also runs Europe's largest convention centre, the ICC [Internationale-Congress-Centrum].

放送塔   ICC ▷

ベルリンのシンボルには「ウドの大木」というあだ名の付いた放送塔もある。1924年から26年にかけてハインリッヒ・シュトラウマーにより設計され、第三回ドイツ放送展覧会の開催に伴って造られたものである。ベルリンはラジオ放送発祥の地である。1923年10月23日、初めてのラジオ放送がポツダム通りのボックスハウスから放送された。ベルリン見本市には面積16万平方メートルのメッセ会場が利用され、同時にヨーロッパで最も大きなベルリン国際会議場 ICC としても使われている。

View from the Funkturm / 森林舞台 / Forest Theatre / 森のステージ

从柏林无线电台上放眼四望,其景色会深深地吸引住游客。广阔的视野,无尽的城区,漫长宽阔的街道、河流、湖泊以及星罗棋布的绿色区域,这里可将一个世界城市的魅力尽收眼底。图上人们可以看到夏洛滕堡城区以及作为绿洲的八百米长的里茨恩湖。镶嵌在穆艾伦大峡谷中一块盆地上的森林舞台是举办交响乐(古典、摇滚以及流行音乐)和播放电影的场所,柏林的森林舞台属于世界上深受喜爱的露天舞台之一。

The view from the Funkturm is breathtaking. It encompasses a seemingly never-ending urban landscape with long, wide streets, rivers and lakes, dappled with green open spaces. In the picture we see. – The Forest Theatre, set in a basin in the Murelle gorge, is a venue for concerts (classical, rock, pop) and films, and has an international reputation as one of the most popular open-air theatres.

放送塔からの眺めは観光客の誰をも圧倒する。長く伸びた大通りが走る都会風の市街区、川、湖、散在する緑地帯などのパノラマが展開される。まさに世界都市のもつ魅力だ。写真に見えるのは、シャルロッテンブルク地区と長さ800メートルの緑のオアシス、リーツェン湖。ムレレン峡の盆地の中に埋まっている「森のステージ」では、クラシック音楽をはじめ、ロック、ポップスなどのコンサートが開催されたり、映画が上映されている。国際的にも大変人気のある野外ステージのひとつである。

柏林的特雷普托和泰格尔 / Berlin-Treptow and Tegel / 行楽地ベルリン・トレプトフとテーゲル
哈维尔湖区的湖滨浴场 / Beach at Wannsee / ヴァン湖の遊泳砂浜

和暖的季节,柏林人都愿意周末到绿色原野中去。许多柏林人去特雷普托公园或施普雷河畔蒂尔加滕公园中的绿色园林中按营扎寨、进行烧烤,也有许多柏林人搭乘郊游游船去到米格勒湖或万湖等城市周边地区远足,在那充满乡村风味的田园景色中,游客们不仅可以戏水游泳,还可上饭店或去娱乐消遣。在施普雷河和哈维尔河许多河道上,游客们可搭乘游轮沿着历史老城和新城随心所欲地环游柏林。

At weekends during the summer season, the people of Berlin flock out into Berlin's extensive green belt. While many Berliners set up barbecues in the idyllic gardens of Treptow Park or unwind in the huge Tiergarten park on the Spree, others take the steamer which transports them to the outskirts of the city, as far as the lakes of Muggelsee and Wannsee. The Spree and Havel canals provide Berlin with a network of numerous waterways which are very popular with tourists wishing to explore the sights of the city by boat.

暖かい季節がやってくると、ベルリン市民は週末を利用して緑の自然の中へ出かけて行く。シュプレー河畔のトレプトフやティーアーガルテンの芝生地でバーベキューをするベルリンっ子もいれば、郊外のミュッゲル湖やヴァン湖への遊覧船の行楽を楽しむ人達もたくさんいる。牧歌的な景色に囲まれて泳ぐこともできれば、レストラン、娯楽も十分にある。ベルリン市内ではシュプレー河、ハーフェル河の水路を往来する河上遊覧船で歴史的かつモダンなベルリンの市内観光を楽しむことができる。

哈维尔湖区的孔雀岛 / Peacock Island in the Havel Lakes / ハーフェル河の孔雀島

柏林是一座绿色的城市。柏林赢得这一美誉不仅是因为道路两旁绿树成荫，还得益于它所拥有的许多森林。万维河湖区是由几个相邻的湖泊组成的，其中最著名的要数万湖。通俗歌曲所咏唱的万湖湖滨浴场几乎已成了一个传奇。多水的地方也一定会有水上运动员的踪迹。各种项目的无数水上运动协会在米格勒湖、哈维尔湖或在湖区的某一流域拥有自己的船坞和协会会。

Berlin is a green city. Not only its tree-lined streets, but also many woods, have helped to establish this reputation. The Havel really is a string of lakes, Wannsee being the most famous one. This lake, which is featured in popular songs, has almost become a legend. With so much water, it is clear that aquatic sports play an important role. There are numerous clubs of all kinds which have their boats and club-houses on the Müggelsee, the lakes of the Havel or one of the others bodies of water.

ベルリンは緑のあふれる街。街路樹はもちろん、たくさんの森が林立しているので緑の町として有名になった。ハーフェル河は元々たくさんの湖が数珠つなぎになったもので、ヴァン湖はその中でも最もよく知られている。この湖はヒット曲にも歌われていて、ほとんど伝説のようになっている。満々と水をたたえた湖は、ウォータースポーツのファンに大人気だ。ミュッゲル湖、ハーフェル河、河川沿いには、ヨットハウスやクラブ・ハウスを持つ水上スポーツクラブが数え切れないほどある。

图片来源 / TABLE OF ILLUSTRATIONS / 写真紹介

Seiten:

Horst Ziethen	1, 13, 15, 17(6) 20, 21, 22, 23, 24, 25, 26, 29, 32,
	34, 35, 36, 38, 39, 40, 41 (4), 42 (2), 45, 46 (4),
	52, 53 (2l.), 54/55 (5), 57, 58, 59, 61, 64, 65,
	66, 67, 68, 70 (2), 71, Titel- und Rücktitelbilder
Fotoservice Weber	27, 33 (2), 49(4), 54/55 (3)
Das Luftbildarchiv	37, 67, 72
Zenit / Langrock	30/31, 56
Photoagentur Peters	51 (b-d), 53 (2.r.)
Fotoagentur H.Lade	14, 19

Zenit / Böning 16; Punctum-Fotografie S.18, 60; Herbert Schlemmer S. 28; Berliner Mauergrafik©Gerd Glanze/Graffiti von Christian „Lake" Wahle S. 43; Werner Huthmacher S. 44; Hildegard Ziethen S. 47 (4); Friedrichstadt-Palast S. 48; Zefa S.50; DPA, Berlin S. 51 (a); Verwaltung Staatl. Schlösser u. Gärten, Schloss Charlottenburg S.62; Archiv Preußischer Kulturbesitz S.63; HB-Verlag S.69;

地图 / Mention of sources used / 地図

<u>Vorsatzseiten:</u> aktuelle Kartengrafik Berlin-City von Bien und Giersch, Projektagentur GmbH;
Grafik: © Verlag Terra Nostra/Ruben Atoyan
<u>Nachsatzseiten:</u> Berlin um 1900 von Bien und Giersch, Projektagentur GmbH, Berlin

---

双页的补充文字: 大约一九零零年的柏林 ▷▷
Trailer double side: BERLIN around 1900
追加見開き頁: 1900年頃のベルリン